Measuring Up®

to the New York
Common Core

PeoplesEducation.com

Peoples
Education
Your partner in student success®

Chief Development Officer: Michael Urban

Vice President, Curriculum and Development: Elisa Eiger

Vice President of Sales and Marketing: Victoria Ameer Kiely

Associate Vice President of Marketing: Angela Glock

Director of Project Management: Lynne Naylor

Editorial Development: Words & Numbers

Editor: Joanne Willard

Copy Editor: Shelly Rawson

Development Services Controller: Jason Grasso

Director, Asset Management: Kristine Liebman

Development Services Assistant: Amy Priddy Wierzbicki

Manager, User Experience: Jennifer Tully

Senior Production Manager: Steven Genzano

Production: Planman Technologies

Cover Design: Joe Guerrero, Todd Kochakji

Acknowledgments:
p. 151, photograph, Copyright © iStockphoto

Your partner in student success®

Copyright © 2013
Peoples Education, Inc.
299 Market Street
Saddle Brook, New Jersey 07663

ISBN 978-1-61526-644-9

Manufactured in Massachusetts in December 2012 by Bradford & Bigelow, Inc.

Printed in the United States of America.

10   9   8   7   6   5   4   3   2   1

Table of Contents

Chapter 1   Foundational Skills

Chapter 2   Fourth-Grade Language Skills

Chapter 2   Fourth-Grade Language Skills (continued)

Chapter 3   Reading Literature

Chapter 4 Reading Informational Texts

Chapter 5   Writing

Your teacher may choose to assign practice tests for this program to check your learning.

Table of Reading Selections

Lesson	Reading Passage	Type				Curricular Connection	Word Count	Reading Level
		Fiction	Nonfiction	Literary	Informational			
1	Josie stared down in astonishment…	✓		✓			138	645
2	The *Titanic*, possibly the most…		✓		✓	History	101	750
3	The Play's the Thing		✓		✓	Music/Arts	120	810
4	A Big Change in Photography		✓		✓	Science	104	830
4	A Dangerous Job		✓		✓	Social Studies	110	870
5	The Mystery of the Old House	✓		✓			60	710
5	It was a cold, snowy night…	✓		✓			99	720
6	A Perfect Part	✓		✓		Music/Arts	274	790
8	Food for Thought	✓		✓		Health	130	570
11	The Twin Prank	✓		✓			208	800
12	The New Neighbor	✓		✓			102	840
12	Lost in the Museum	✓		✓		Science	178	820
13	The Social Studies Report	✓		✓		Social Studies	90	950
13	The Night Prowler	✓		✓			192	810
14	The Dancing Spider	✓		✓			104	820
14	Avalanche!	✓		✓		Science	205	790
15	Vote for Tim!	✓		✓		Civics	124	820
15	Cleanup Crew	✓		✓		Science, Civics	182	790
16	City Winter	✓		✓		Geography	101	830
16	The Crossing	✓		✓		History	237	950
17	The Second Labor of Hercules	✓		✓		Literature, Social Studies	110	970
17	Reynard and the Fish (a folktale from Europe)	✓		✓		Literature, Social Studies	114	800
17	Turtle's Rescue (a folktale from India)	✓		✓		Literature, Social Studies	99	830
18	Snow Joy	✓		✓		Sports	115	890
18	Surprise!	✓		✓			229	860
19	All Together Now	✓		✓		Sports	158	820

Lesson	Reading Passage	Type				Curricular Connection	Word Count	Reading Level
		Fiction	Nonfiction	Literary	Informational			
19	The Woodman and the Axe	✓		✓		Literature	126	920
19	The Runaway Tennis Ball	✓		✓		Sports	133	850
20	from *Alice in Wonderland* by Lewis Carroll	✓		✓		Literature	94	700
20	from "Casey at the Bat" by Ernest Thayer	✓		✓		Literature	130	880
20	from "No Joy in Mudville"	✓		✓		Literature	36	n/a
21	The Long Way Home	✓		✓			160	950
21	Soccer Showdown	✓		✓		Sports	229	930
22	Be a Good Citizen!		✓		✓	Civics	162	890
22	Watch Out for Poison Ivy!		✓		✓	Science	275	850
23	All About Raptors		✓		✓	Science	272	940
23	Turkey Vultures—Fact and Fiction!		✓		✓	Science	302	950
24	Learning a Second Language		✓		✓	Social Studies	237	960
24	Soap, Beautiful Soap!		✓		✓	History	175	970
25	Sleep-Deprived or Spoiled?		✓		✓	Science	272	980
25	Travelin' Shoes		✓		✓	Science	319	970
26	from "The Highwayman" by Alfred Noyes	✓		✓		Literature	108	n/a
26	from "Grandfather's Clock" by Henry Clay Work	✓		✓		Literature	227	1260
27	Owl Pellets		✓		✓	Science	260	940
27	The Inside Story		✓		✓	Science	261	880
28	Develop the Savings Habit!		✓		✓	Economics	357	970
28	Creatures of the Deep: Giant Tube Worms		✓		✓	Science	274	980
29	It's Cloudy!		✓		✓	Science	141	870
29	Time Line of Events Leading to the American Revolution		✓		✓	History	266	n/a
30	The Bicycle Accident	✓		✓			195	770
30	Arriving at Ellis Island	✓			✓	History	363	950
31	The Negro Leagues/Jackie Robinson		✓		✓	History, Sports	281	940
31	Western Screech Owls		✓		✓	Science	329	970
32	The Vocabulary of Space		✓		✓	Science	179	910
32	A Hike in the Mojave Desert		✓		✓	Science	211	930
36	The Fox and the Stork by Aesop	✓		✓			184	660

Correlation to the New York State Common Core Learning Standards

New York State Common Core Learning Standards	Lessons
College and Career Readiness Anchor Standards for Reading, Grades K-5	
Key Ideas and Details	
CCR.R.1 Read closely to determine what the text says explicitly and to make logical inferences from it; cite specific textual evidence when writing or speaking to support conclusions drawn from the text.	12, 13, 23, 24
CCR.R.2 Determine central ideas or themes of a text and analyze their development; summarize the key supporting details and ideas.	14, 19, 22, 23, 25
CCR.R.3 Analyze how and why individuals, events, and ideas develop and interact over the course of a text.	15, 16, 17, 27
Craft and Structure	
CCR.R.4 Interpret words and phrases as they are used in a text, including determining technical, connotative, and figurative meanings, and analyze how specific word choices shape meaning or tone.	21, 32
CCR.R.5 Analyze the structure of texts, including how specific sentences, paragraphs, and larger portions of the text (e.g., a section, chapter, scene, or stanza) relate to each other and the whole.	26
CCR.R.6 Assess how point of view or purpose shapes the content and style of a text.	18, 30
Integration of Knowledge and Ideas	
CCR.R.7 Integrate and evaluate content presented in diverse media and formats, including visually and quantitatively, as well as in words.	20, 29
CCR.R.8 Delineate and evaluate the argument and specific claims in a text, including the validity of the reasoning as well as the relevance and sufficiency of the evidence.	28
CCR.R.9 Analyze how two or more texts address similar themes or topics in order to build knowledge or to compare the approaches the authors take.	19, 31
Range of Reading and Level of Text Complexity	
CCR.R.10 Read and comprehend complex literary and informational texts independently and proficiently.	4, 11
Responding to Literature	
CCR.R.11 Respond to literature by employing knowledge of literary language, textual features, and forms to read and comprehend, reflect upon, and interpret literary texts from a variety of genres and a wide spectrum of American and world cultures.	11, 19, 36
Reading Standards for Literature, Grade 4	
Key Ideas and Details	
RL.4.1 Refer to details and examples in a text when explaining what the text says explicitly and when drawing inferences from the text.	12, 13

> **Key to Lesson References:**
> **GUM** = Grammar, Usage, and Mechanics Handbook (numbered by Mini-Lesson)
> **SLH** = Speaking and Listening Handbook (numbered by Mini-Lesson)

New York State Common Core Learning Standards	Lessons
RL.4.2 Determine a theme of a story, drama, or poem from details in the text; summarize the text.	14, 19
RL.4.3 Describe in depth a character, setting, or event in a story or drama, drawing on specific details in the text (e.g., a character's thoughts, words, or actions).	15, 16, 17
Craft and Structure	
RL.4.4 Determine the meaning of words and phrases as they are used in a text, including those that allude to significant characters found in mythology (e.g., Herculean).	21
RL.4.5 Explain major differences between poems, drama, and prose, and refer to the structural elements of poems (e.g., verse, rhythm, meter) and drama (e.g., casts of characters, settings, descriptions, dialogue, stage directions) when writing or speaking about a text.	11
RL.4.6 Compare and contrast the point of view from which different stories are narrated, including the difference between first- and third-person narrations.	18
Integration of Knowledge and Ideas	
RL.4.7 Make connections between the text of a story or drama and a visual or oral presentation of the text, identifying where each version reflects specific descriptions and directions in the text.	20
RL.4.9 Compare and contrast the treatment of similar themes and topics (e.g., opposition of good and evil) and patterns of events (e.g., the quest) in stories, myths, and traditional literature from different cultures.	17, 19
Range of Reading and Level of Text Complexity	
RL.4.10 By the end of the year, read and comprehend literature, including stories, dramas, and poetry, in the grades 4–5 text complexity band proficiently, with scaffolding as needed at the high end of the range.	11, 21
Responding to Literature	
RL.4.11 Recognize, interpret, and make connections in narratives, poetry, and drama to other texts, ideas, cultural perspectives, personal events, and situations.	12, 15, 36
a. Self-select text based upon personal preferences.	15, 36
Reading Standards for Informational Text, Grade 4	
Key Ideas and Details	
RI.4.1 Refer to details and examples in a text when explaining what the text says explicitly and when drawing inferences from the text.	23, 24
RI.4.2 Determine the main idea of a text and explain how it is supported by key details; summarize the text.	22, 23, 25
RI.4.3 Explain events, procedures, ideas, or concepts in a historical, scientific, or technical text, including what happened and why, based on specific information in the text.	27
Craft and Structure	
RI.4.4 Determine the meaning of general academic and domain-specific words or phrases in a text relevant to a grade 4 topic or subject area.	32
RI.4.5 Describe the overall structure (e.g., chronology, comparison, cause/effect, problem/solution) of events, ideas, concepts, or information in a text or part of a text.	26
RI.4.6 Compare and contrast a firsthand and secondhand account of the same event or topic; describe the differences in focus and the information provided.	30

New York State Common Core Learning Standards	Lessons
Integration of Knowledge and Ideas	
RI.4.7 Interpret information presented visually, orally, or quantitatively (e.g., in charts, graphs, diagrams, time lines, animations, or interactive elements on Web pages) and explain how the information contributes to an understanding of the text in which it appears.	29
RI.4.8 Explain how an author uses reasons and evidence to support particular points in a text.	28
RI.4.9 Integrate information from two texts on the same topic in order to write or speak about the subject knowledgeably.	31
Range of Reading and Level of Text Complexity	
RI.4.10 By the end of year, read and comprehend informational texts, including history/social studies, science, and technical texts, in the grades 4–5 text complexity band proficiently, with scaffolding as needed at the high end of the range.	22, 32
Reading Standards: Foundational Skills, Grade 4	
Phonics and Word Recognition	
RF.4.3 Know and apply grade-level phonics and word analysis skills in decoding words.	1, 2
a. Use combined knowledge of all letter-sound correspondences, syllabication patterns, and morphology (e.g., roots and affixes) to read accurately unfamiliar multisyllabic words in context and out of context.	1, 2
Fluency	
RF.4.4 Read with sufficient accuracy and fluency to support comprehension.	3, 4, 5
a. Read on-level text with purpose and understanding.	4
b. Read on-level prose and poetry orally with accuracy, appropriate rate, and expression on successive readings	5
c. Use context to confirm or self-correct word recognition and understanding, rereading as necessary.	3
College and Career Readiness Anchor Standards for Writing, Grades K-5	
Text Types and Purposes	
CCR.W.1 Write arguments to support claims in an analysis of substantive topics or texts, using valid reasoning and relevant and sufficient evidence.	33
CCR.W.2 Write informative/explanatory texts to examine and convey complex ideas and information clearly and accurately through the effective selection, organization, and analysis of content.	34
CCR.W.3 Write narratives to develop real or imagined experiences or events using effective technique, well-chosen details, and well-structured event sequences.	35
Production and Distribution of Writing	
CCR.W.4 Produce clear and coherent writing in which the development, organization, and style are appropriate to task, purpose, and audience.	33, 34, 35
CCR.W.5 Develop and strengthen writing as needed by planning, revising, editing, rewriting, or trying a new approach.	33, 34, 35
CCR.W.6 Use technology, including the Internet, to produce and publish writing and to interact and collaborate with others.	33, 35

New York State Common Core Learning Standards	Lessons
Research to Build and Present Knowledge	
CCR.W.7 Conduct short as well as more sustained research projects based on focused questions, demonstrating understanding of the subject under investigation.	33, 34
CCR.W.8 Gather relevant information from multiple print and digital sources, assess the credibility and accuracy of each source, and integrate the information while avoiding plagiarism.	33, 34
CCR.W.9 Draw evidence from literary or informational texts to support analysis, reflection, and research.	33, 34
Range of Writing	
CCR.W.10 Write routinely over extended time frames (time for research, reflection, and revision) and shorter time frames (a single sitting or a day or two) for a range of tasks, purposes, and audiences.	33, 34, 35
Responding to Literature	
CCR.W.11 Develop personal, cultural, textual, and thematic connections within and across genres as they respond to texts through written, digital, and oral presentations, employing a variety of media and genres	36
Writing Standards, Grade 4	
Text Types and Purposes	
W.4.1 Write opinion pieces on topics or texts, supporting a point of view with reasons.	33, 35
a. Introduce a topic or text clearly, state an opinion, and create an organizational structure in which related ideas are grouped to support the writer's purpose.	27, 33
b. Provide reasons that support the opinion.	26, 33
c. Link opinion and reasons using words and phrases (e.g., *for instance, in order to, in addition*).	33, 35
d. Provide a concluding statement or section.	33, 34, 35
W.4.2 Write informative/explanatory texts to examine a topic and convey ideas and information clearly.	23, 34
a. Introduce a topic clearly and group related information in paragraphs and sections; include formatting (e.g., headings), illustrations, and multimedia when useful to aiding comprehension.	24, 29, 34
b. Develop the topic with facts, definitions, concrete details, quotations, or other information and examples related to the topic.	23, 30, 34
c. Link ideas within categories of information using words and phrases (e.g., *another, for example, also, because*).	22, 34
d. Use precise language and domain-specific vocabulary to inform about or explain the topic.	28, 34
e. Provide a concluding statement or section related to the information or explanation presented.	25, 34
W.4.3 Write narratives to develop real or imagined experiences or events using effective technique, descriptive details, and clear event sequences.	35
a. Orient the reader by establishing a situation and introducing a narrator and/or characters; organize an event sequence that unfolds naturally.	35
b. Use dialogue and description to develop experiences and events or show the responses of characters to situations.	35

New York State Common Core Learning Standards	Lessons
c. Use a variety of transitional words and phrases to manage the sequence of events.	34, 35
d. Use concrete words and phrases and sensory details to convey experiences and events precisely.	31, 32, 35
e. Provide a conclusion that follows from the narrated experiences or events.	35
Production and Distribution of Writing	
W.4.4 With guidance and support from adults, produce writing in which the development and organization are appropriate to task and purpose.	33, 34, 35
W.4.5 With guidance and support from peers and adults, develop and strengthen writing as needed by planning, revising, and editing.	33, 34, 35
W.4.6 With some guidance and support from adults, use technology, including the Internet, to produce and publish writing as well as to interact and collaborate with others; demonstrate sufficient command of keyboarding skills to type a minimum of one page in a single sitting.	34, 35
Research to Build and Present Knowledge	
W.4.7 Conduct short research projects that build knowledge through investigation of different aspects of a topic.	34
W.4.8 Recall relevant information from experiences or gather relevant information from print and digital sources; take notes and categorize information, and provide a list of sources.	34
W.4.9 Draw evidence from literary or informational texts to support analysis, reflection, and research.	33, 34
a. Apply *grade 4 Reading standards* to literature (e.g., "Describe in depth a character, setting, or event in a story or drama, drawing on specific details in the text [e.g., a character's thoughts, words, or actions].").	33
b. Apply *grade 4 Reading standards* to informational texts (e.g., "Explain how an author uses reasons and evidence to support particular points in a text").	34
Range of Writing	
W.4.10 Write routinely over extended time frames (time for research, reflection, and revision) and shorter time frames (a single sitting or a day or two) for a range of discipline-specific tasks, purposes, and audiences.	34, 35
Responding to Literature	
W.4.11 Create and present a poem, narrative, play, art work, or literary review in response to a particular author or theme studied in class.	35, 36
College and Career Readiness Anchor Standards for Speaking and Listening, Grades K-5	
Comprehension and Collaboration	
CCR.SL.1 Prepare for and participate effectively in a range of conversations and collaborations with diverse partners, building on others' ideas and expressing their own clearly and persuasively.	8, 11, 12, 13, 14, 16, 18, 19, 20, 21, SLH 2
CCR.SL.2 Integrate and evaluate information presented in diverse media and formats, including visually, quantitatively, and orally.	SLH 2, 5
CCR.SL.3 Evaluate a speaker's point of view, reasoning, and use of evidence and rhetoric.	SLH 3, 6

New York State Common Core Learning Standards	Lessons
Presentation of Knowledge and Ideas	
CCR.SL.4 Present information, findings, and supporting evidence such that listeners can follow the line of reasoning and the organization, development, and style are appropriate to task, purpose, and audience.	SLH 5, 6
CCR.SL.5 Make strategic use of digital media and visual displays of data to express information and enhance understanding of presentations.	SLH 4
CCR.SL.6 Adapt speech to a variety of contexts and communicative tasks, demonstrating command of formal English when indicated or appropriate.	SLH 1, 2
Speaking and Listening Standards, Grade 4	
Comprehension and Collaboration	
SL.4.1 Engage effectively in a range of collaborative discussions (one-on-one, in groups, and teacher-led) with diverse partners on grade 4 topics and texts, building on others' ideas and expressing their own clearly.	1, 4, 5, 8, 23, SLH
a. Come to discussions prepared, having read or studied required material; explicitly draw on that preparation and other information known about the topic to explore ideas under discussion.	24, SLH 1
b. Follow agreed-upon rules for discussions and carry out assigned roles.	30, SLH 1, 2
c. Pose and respond to specific questions to clarify or follow up on information, and make comments that contribute to the discussion and link to the remarks of others.	23, 31, SLH 2
d. Review the key ideas expressed and explain their own ideas and understanding in light of the discussion.	25, SLH 3
e. Seek to understand and communicate with individuals from different perspectives and cultural backgrounds.	30, 36
SL.4.2 Paraphrase portions of a text read aloud or information presented in diverse media and formats, including visually, quantitatively, and orally.	26, SLH 5
SL.4.3 Identify the reasons and evidence a speaker provides to support particular points.	4, 22, SLH 6
Presentation of Knowledge and Ideas	
SL.4.4 Report on a topic or text, tell a story, or recount an experience in an organized manner, using appropriate facts and relevant, descriptive details to support main ideas or themes; speak clearly at an understandable pace.	27, 32, SLH 4
SL.4.5 Add audio recordings and visual displays to presentations when appropriate to enhance the development of main ideas or themes.	28, 29, SLH 4
SL.4.6 Differentiate between contexts that call for formal English (e.g., presenting ideas) and situations where informal discourse is appropriate (e.g., small-group discussion); use formal English when appropriate to task and situation.	SLH 4
College and Career Readiness Anchor Standards for Language, Grades K-5	
Conventions of Standard English	
CCR.L.1 Demonstrate command of the conventions of standard English grammar and usage when writing or speaking.	GUM
CCR.L.2 Demonstrate command of the conventions of standard English capitalization, punctuation, and spelling when writing.	GUM

New York State Common Core Learning Standards	Lessons
Knowledge of Language	
CCR.L.3 Apply knowledge of language to understand how language functions in different contexts, to make effective choices for meaning or style, and to comprehend more fully when reading or listening.	2, 4, 6, 8, 10
Vocabulary Acquisition and Use	
CCR.L.4 Determine or clarify the meaning of unknown and multiple-meaning words and phrases by using context clues, analyzing meaningful word parts, and consulting general and specialized reference materials, as appropriate.	2, 3, 6, 10
CCR.L.5 Demonstrate understanding of figurative language, word relationships, and nuances in word meanings.	7, 8, 9
CCR.L.6 Acquire and use accurately a range of general academic and domain-specific words and phrases sufficient for reading, writing, speaking, and listening at the college and career readiness level; demonstrate independence in gathering vocabulary knowledge when encountering an unknown term important to comprehension or expression.	2, 4, 6, 8, 10
Language Standards, Grade 4	
Conventions of Standard English	
L.4.1 Demonstrate command of the conventions of standard English grammar and usage when writing or speaking.	GUM
a. Use relative pronouns (*who, whose, whom, which, that*) and relative adverbs (*where, when, why*).	GUM 1, 2
b. Form and use the progressive (e.g., *I was walking; I am walking; I will be walking*) verb tenses.	GUM 3
c. Use modal auxiliaries (e.g., *can, may, must*) to convey various conditions.	GUM 4
d. Order adjectives within sentences according to conventional patterns (e.g., *a small red bag* rather than *a red small bag*).	GUM 5
e. Form and use prepositional phrases.	GUM 6
f. Produce complete sentences, recognizing and correcting inappropriate fragments and run-ons.	GUM 7, 8
g. Correctly use frequently confused words (e.g., *to, too, two; there, their*).	GUM 9
L.4.2 Demonstrate command of the conventions of standard English capitalization, punctuation, and spelling when writing.	GUM
a. Use correct capitalization.	GUM 10, 11, 12
b. Use commas and quotation marks to mark direct speech and quotations from a text.	GUM 13
c. Use a comma before a coordinating conjunction in a compound sentence.	GUM 14
d. Spell grade-appropriate words correctly, consulting references as needed.	GUM 15
Knowledge of Language	
L.4.3 Use knowledge of language and its conventions when writing, speaking, reading, or listening.	GUM
a. Choose words and phrases to convey ideas precisely.	35
b. Choose punctuation for effect.	GUM

New York State Common Core Learning Standards	Lessons
c. Differentiate between contexts that call for formal English (e.g., presenting ideas) and situations where informal discourse is appropriate (e.g., small-group discussion).	SLH 4, 6
Vocabulary Acquisition and Use	
L.4.4 Determine or clarify the meaning of unknown and multiple-meaning words and phrases based on *grade 4 reading and content*, choosing flexibly from a range of strategies.	6
a. Use context (e.g., definitions, examples, or restatements in text) as a clue to the meaning of a word or phrase.	3
b. Use common, grade-appropriate Greek and Latin affixes and roots as clues to the meaning of a word (e.g., *telegraph, photograph, autograph*).	2
c. Consult reference materials (e.g., dictionaries, glossaries, thesauruses), both print and digital, to find the pronunciation and determine or clarify the precise meaning of key words and phrases.	10
L.4.5 Demonstrate understanding of word relationships and nuances in word meanings.	7, 8, 9
a. Explain the meaning of simple similes and metaphors (e.g., *as pretty as a picture*) in context.	7
b. Recognize and explain the meaning of common idioms, adages, and proverbs.	8
c. Demonstrate understanding of words by relating them to their opposites (antonyms) and to words with similar but not identical meanings (synonyms).	9
L.4.6 Acquire and use accurately grade-appropriate general academic and domain-specific words and phrases, including those that signal precise actions, emotions, or states of being (e.g., *quizzed, whined, stammered*) and that are basic to a particular topic (e.g., *wildlife, conservation*, and *endangered* when discussing animal preservation).	2, 4, 6, 8, 10

to the
New York Common Core

To the Student:

It's never too soon to prepare for your future. The same goes for learning the New York State Common Core Learning Standards for your grade level. Learning these standards will help you succeed in your academic pursuits and prepare for college and your career.

The lessons in this book will help you learn all the New York State Common Core Learning Standards for English Language Arts. This book is divided into five chapters. Each one focuses on a different set of skills that you need to read, write, speak, and listen critically. Each chapter matches one of the strands, or main categories, in the New York State Common Core Learning Standards for English Language Arts:

- Reading Literature
- Reading Informational Text
- Reading: Foundational Skills
- Language
- Writing

Each chapter includes:

- A review of skills and key vocabulary
- Real-world examples
- Stories and nonfiction passages that stretch your thinking
- A variety of activities and questions that allow you to show your learning
- Practice with multiple-choice, short-answer, and extended-response questions
- Kick It Up activities that will boost your learning to the next level

Language and *Speaking and Listening* skills are woven into the reading and writing lessons. However, you'll also get a chance to focus on the standards that make up these two strands in the "Grammar, Usage, and Mechanics Handbook" and the "Speaking and Listening Handbook." The handbooks contain mini-lessons to help you build your communications skills.

The lessons in this book will help you build your English Language Arts skills and improve your thinking skills. The lessons may seem challenging at first, but keep at it and you will be a success!

Have a great school year!

Peoples
Education
Your partner in student success®

to the
New York Common Core

To Parents and Families:

Peoples Education has created this book to help your child master the New York State Common Core Learning Standards for English Language Arts. The New York State Common Core Learning Standards, a set of K–12 grade-specific expectations that were developed by a consortium of states and coordinated by the National Governors Association and the Council of Chief State School Officers, define what it means for students to be college- and career-ready in the 21st century.

Each chapter in this book is focused on a different set of skills, matching the strands, or main categories, in the New York State Common Core Learning Standards for English Language Arts:

- Reading Literature
- Reading Informational Text
- Reading: Foundational Skills
- Language
- Writing

Each chapter includes:

- A review of skills and key vocabulary
- Stories and/or nonfiction passages that stretch your child's thinking
- A variety of activities and questions that allow your child to show his or her skill comprehension
- Practice with writing prompts and multiple-choice, short-answer, and extended-response items
- Kick It Up activities to boost your child's learning to the next level

Language and *Speaking and Listening* skills are woven into the reading and writing lessons. In addition, the "Grammar, Usage, and Mechanics Handbook" and the "Speaking and Listening Handbook" contain mini-lessons to help build your child's communications skills.

For success in school and the real world, your child needs a solid English language arts foundation, and your involvement is crucial to that success. Here are some suggestions:

- Read aloud to your child. Find a quiet place to read. If the book has pictures, talk about them. As your child listens, ask him or her to anticipate what will happen next. Talk about the characters and what happens to them.
- Treat reading as a pleasure. Give books as presents and show that you like to receive them, too. Respect each other's private reading time.
- Take pride in your child's writing. Post it on the refrigerator. Keep a scrapbook. Write cards to family and friends together.
- As you listen to television or radio and watch movies, engage in a discussion about what you hear and see. Question information. Talk about how the information relates to your own experience. Ask for your child's reactions.

Get involved! Work with us this year to ensure your child's success. Reading, writing, speaking, listening, and language skills are essential both inside and outside of school. They will give pleasure throughout your child's life.

What's Inside: A Lesson Guide

Lessons in this worktext are divided into three sections in which the New York State Common Core Learning Standards are introduced and explained, applied, and independently practiced.

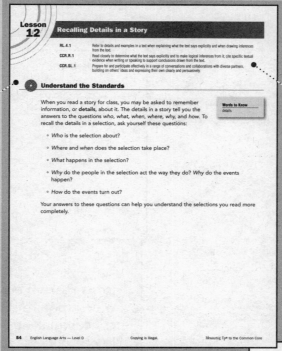

Understand the Standards introduces and explains the standards. The Words to Know box highlights important terms and vocabulary included in the lesson.

The New York State Common Core Learning Standards on which the lesson focuses are clearly identified at the beginning of every lesson.

Includes lessons for New York Standard 11: Responding to Literature

Guided Instruction features a reading selection with Guided Questions that help students apply the standards to the text. The guided reading selection may be followed by additional questions that challenge students to think about the text in deeper, more complex ways.

Guided Questions check comprehension and also help students think critically about the reading selection.

On Your Own

consists of items that challenge students to apply what they have learned and demonstrate their mastery of the standards.

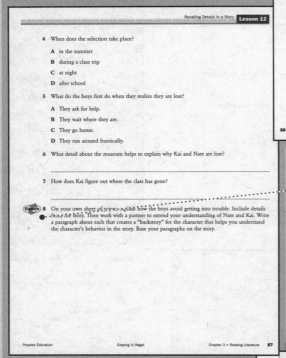

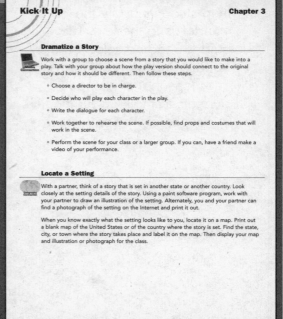

Icons make it easy to identify Elevate items, which require students to use higher-order critical thinking skills. Icons are also used to call out Critical Thinking exercises, opportunities for Collaborative Learning, and connections to media, school subjects, and real-world topics.

Kick It Up

At the end of each chapter, Kick It Up **project-based activities** provide a cumulative review of skills. Each Kick It Up activity is designed to challenge students with tasks that require deep thinking and skills such as research, collaboration, problem solving, using technology, and writing.

Lesson 1

Reviewing Phonics

RF.4.3	Know and apply grade-level phonics and word analysis skills in decoding words. **a.** Use combined knowledge of all letter-sound correspondences, syllabication patterns, and morphology to read accurately unfamiliar multisyllabic words in context and out of context.
SL.4.1	Engage effectively in a range of collaborative discussions with diverse partners on grade 4 topics and texts, building on others' ideas and expressing their own clearly.

 ## Understand the Standards

Imagine that you are reading a story. You come across this sentence:

> After the award ceremony, Mark asked for the winner's autograph.

Words to Know
pronounce
syllables

You might not recognize the words *ceremony* and *autograph*. If you don't have a dictionary or glossary to check, use what you know about letters and sounds to figure out how to **pronounce**, or say, the words. You might know the words' meanings once you hear them.

Use these steps to figure out a new word:

- **Break it into parts.** Start by breaking a long word into smaller words or syllables. *Autograph* is made up of two smaller world parts: *auto* and *graph*. You can take it a step further and break it into groups of letters called **syllables**: au•to•graph. Then you can move on to the next step to figure out how to say each syllable.

- **Link sounds to letters.** Sound out each syllable or small part of a word. Review words you know that have the same letters. If you know how to say *automobile*, you know how to say the first two syllables of *autograph*. Think about spelling rules to figure out which sound a letter makes. If you know that *c* usually makes an /s/ sound when it comes before an *e*, then you know that *ceremony* starts with an /s/ sound.

- **Say it aloud.** Once you break the word into parts and link sounds to the letters, put the word back together and say each sound aloud. Repeat the word until it flows naturally.

Guided Instruction

Syllables can be made up of a single vowel, two vowels together, or a group of consonants and vowels. Knowing how letters work together helps you divide words into syllables.

Example: Patty had **enough** time to take a walk before dinner.

Think: I know that the letters *g* and *h* often work together to make the /f/ sound. The *o* and *u* sometimes work together to make an /uh/ sound, as in *tough* and *rough*. I can use this to break up *enough* into two parts: e•nough.

Besides the /uh/ sound, what else do you notice about *tough* and *rough*?

_____

Complete and discuss these activities.

1. Break these words into syllables.

   telephone   **reason**   **earthquake**

   _____

2. Say the word *courage*. Does the *g* make a /g/ or /j/ sound? Write two other words that use the *g* the same way.

   _____

3. Read this sentence.

   The Fourth of July is a national holiday.

   How many syllables does *national* have? Does the *a* in the first syllable make the same sound as the *a* in *clap* or in *cake*?

   _____

4. Read this sentence.

   The cautious children crossed the street after looking in both directions.

   Which words in the sentence have two syllables? Three syllables?

   _____

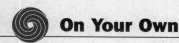 **On Your Own**

Read the passage. Then answer the questions with a partner.

Josie stared down in astonishment. She couldn't believe the sheer number of pieces her mother's favorite vase had shattered into. As she peered at the mess, it was clear that she could never glue it back together. That would simply be impossible. She considered cleaning up the mess and hiding the evidence. It might take weeks for her mom to realize that the vase was missing. Finally, she made a decision about what to do.

"Mom," Josie said, "I have some good news and bad news. Which do you want first?"

Her mother looked puzzled and asked what happened. Josie told her about the broken vase to start and then offered her piggy bank to her mother to buy a new one. Her mother smiled and declined the offer. She told Josie what a great daughter she was.

1 Which words in the first paragraph have the same sound as the *eer* in *sheer*?

_____

2 How many syllables make up *astonishment*? How should the word be divided?

_____

3 Read this sentence.

   That would simply be impossible.

How many syllables make up *impossible*? Which other word in the sentence shares a vowel sound with *impossible*?

_____

4 Which word has the same vowel sound as the first syllable of *daughter—Josie, considered,* or *offered*?

_____

5 Which word has the same long /i/ sound as *hire*?

A prince

B slippery

C stripe

D wrist

6 Which word has the same sound as the sound spelled by the letters *gh* in *cough*?

    A thought

    B tough

    C although

    D fought

7 How many syllables make up the word *subtraction*? How should it be divided?

_____

8 Read the sentence.

    When Jason stepped in the shower, he found a spider by the drain.

    Which word has the same sound as the sound made by the *ow* in *shower*? What is another word with that sound?

_____

 9 On your own sheet of paper, explain the steps you take to figure out the word *entertainment*. Next, discuss with a partner how he or she figured out the word. Then agree on how you would teach another student how to pronounce the word.

RF.4.3	Know and apply grade-level phonics and word analysis skills in decoding words. **a.** Use combined knowledge of all letter-sound correspondences, syllabication patterns, and morphology to read accurately unfamiliar multisyllabic words in context and out of context.
L.4.4	Determine or clarify the meaning of unknown and multiple-meaning words and phrases based on grade 4 reading and content, choosing flexibly from a range of strategies. **b.** Use common, grade-appropriate Greek and Latin affixes and roots as clues to the meaning of a word.
L.4.6	Acquire and use accurately grade-appropriate general academic and domain-specific words and phrases, including those that signal precise actions, emotions, or states of being and that are basic to a particular topic.
CCR.L.3	Apply knowledge of language to understand how language functions in different contexts, to make effective choices for meaning or style, and to comprehend more fully when reading or listening.
CCR.L.4	Determine or clarify the meaning of unknown and multiple-meaning words and phrases by using context clues, analyzing meaningful word parts, and consulting general and specialized reference materials, as appropriate.
CCR.L.6	Acquire and use accurately a range of general academic and domain-specific words and phrases sufficient for reading, writing, speaking, and listening at the college and career readiness level; demonstrate independence in gathering vocabulary knowledge when encountering an unknown term important to comprehension or expression.

Understand the Standards

Imagine you are reading a novel and come across this sentence.

> Kim's idea of **perfection** was a day spent swimming and playing volleyball.

Words to Know
root word
prefix
suffix

The word *perfection* looks familiar, but you aren't quite sure what it means. You might know its root word: *perfect*. If you know the meaning of the suffix *-ion*, you can figure out the new word.

Words are made up of three major parts—prefixes, root words, and suffixes. Knowing the meanings of common word parts can help you figure out new words.

○ A **root word** gives a word's basic meaning. It is the base of a word. Other words can be built by adding parts to this base.

○ A **prefix** is a word part added to the beginning of a root word. Adding a prefix changes a word's meaning.

Word	Prefix	Meaning	New Word	Meaning
monthly	bi-	both, twice	bimonthly	twice a month
large	en- (em-)	to make	enlarge	to make bigger
dairy	non-	not, without	nondairy	without milk/dairy

○ A **suffix** is a word part added to the end of a root word. Adding a suffix changes a word's meaning. It can also change its part of speech.

Word	Suffix	Meaning	New Word	Meaning
collect	-able (-ible)	able to, worthy of	collectible	worthy of collecting
quick	-ly	in a certain way	quickly	in a fast way
govern	-ment	state, quality, act of	government	act of governing

 ## Guided Instruction

When you see a word you don't know, break it into parts. First look for the main part of the word. Think about words you know with that main part. Then see if the word has a prefix or a suffix. Look at this list.

Prefix	Meaning	Suffix	Meaning
mis-	in a wrong way	-ful	full of
pre-	before	-ion	state or condition; act or process
un-	not, opposite	-ness	state of

Read the sentences. Study the underlined word. Use the word parts you have learned in this lesson to complete the activities.

1. **The new cook at the "Mister Chang's" restaurant <u>misread</u> the recipe.**

   What is the main word in *misread*? What does it mean? What does *misread* mean?

   _____

   Why does the word *misspell* have the prefix *mis-* in it but not the word *mister*?

   _____

   _____

2. **Shana's little brother went to <u>preschool</u> today.**

   What two word parts make up *preschool*? What does *preschool* mean?

   _____

3. **Thomas <u>completely</u> forgot about his social studies test.**

   What is the main part of *completely*? What does it mean? What does *completely* mean?

   _____

On Your Own

Read the passage. Use the chart to break apart the underlined words and tell their meanings.

The *Titanic*, possibly the most famous ship in history, set sail in April 1912. The ship was the largest to date and held 2,200 passengers. Excitement was in the air as the *Titanic* left the harbor on April 10. A nonstop trip from England to New York was under way. A popular advertisement encouraged people to travel by sea. Because people believed the ship was unsinkable, lifeboats for only half of the passengers were taken on the trip. But the public was misinformed. The *Titanic* sank on April 15, after hitting an iceberg. That mistake took the lives of 1,572 people.

Word	Prefix	Root Word	Suffix	Meaning
possibly				
nonstop				
advertisement				
unsinkable				
misinformed				

Complete the following activities based on the passage you just read.

1 Which word shares a root with *happiness*?

   A quietness

   B unhappy

   C shape

   D joy

2 If you *pronounce* a word, you say it. What do you do if you *mispronounce* a word?

   A You repeat the word.

   B You do not say the word.

   C You say the word the wrong way.

   D You say the word before another word.

3 Read the sentence.

   When Julia told Raoul a silly story, he said, "That's <u>nonsense</u>!"

What is the root word of *nonsense*? What does the word *nonsense* mean?

_____

_____

4 Divide the word *encouragement* into parts. What does each part mean? What does *encouragement* mean?

_____

_____

5 Use what you know about prefixes, root words, and suffixes to read and define these words.

   biweekly   **dreadful**   **explanation**   **gentleness**   **empower**

On your own sheet of paper, write the meaning of each word and use it in a sentence of your own.

Using Context Clues

RF.4.4	Read with sufficient accuracy and fluency to support comprehension. **c.** Use context to confirm or self-correct word recognition and understanding, rereading as necessary.
L.4.4	Determine or clarify the meaning of unknown and multiple-meaning words and phrases based on grade 4 reading and content, choosing flexibly from a range of strategies. **a.** Use context as a clue to the meaning of a word or phrase.
CCR.L.4	Determine or clarify the meaning of unknown and multiple-meaning words and phrases by using context clues, analyzing meaningful word parts, and consulting general and specialized reference materials, as appropriate.

Understand the Standards

Imagine that you are reading a novel. You come across this paragraph:

> Shane couldn't believe he had been separated from his hiking group. He was lost in the mountains on his own. He knew his first *necessity* was water. He wouldn't last long without it.

You might not know the meaning of *necessity*. The clues in the paragraph can help you figure out the meaning. The writer gives water as an example of a necessity and explains that the character needs this necessity to stay alive. From these clues, you can figure out that a necessity is something that is necessary or needed.

Language Connection

○ The **context** of a word includes all the words and sentences around it. **Context clues** are the words and phrases that give direct hints to the meanings of other words. Context clues come in different forms. For example:

Definitions: The meaning of a word or its synonym is in the text nearby.

> The students had to **distribute**, <u>or hand out</u>, fliers for the class carnival.

Examples: Details and descriptions give examples of a word's meaning.

> The high school student had a hard time deciding on an **occupation**. <u>Working</u> as a <u>lifeguard</u> sounded like fun, but the pay for being a <u>grocery clerk</u> was higher.

Restatements: A word's meaning is described using other, easier words.

> She was **skeptical** when he told her the story. Actually, she <u>really doubted the truth of</u> what he said.

Guided Instruction

Read the passage, then complete the activity.

The Play's the Thing

Music/Arts Connection

Last year a theater company visited town. They planned to stage a <u>production</u> of a popular play. They would put together the sets and rent a space to put on the play. However, they needed actors from the area to complete the cast, so they held <u>auditions</u>, or tryouts, for a week. The people from the neighborhood were not <u>professional</u> actors. They didn't act in plays as their job, but they had fun doing it as a hobby. A <u>distinguished</u>, or well-respected, actor played the lead part. In the end, the <u>performance</u> for the town was not only <u>profitable</u>, but it was also reviewed as <u>outstanding</u>. Not only did it make money, but the actors and crew did a super job.

Guided Questions

Would you like to be involved in the kind of activity described in this passage? Why or why not?

_____

_____

_____

_____

_____

_____

_____

_____

_____

The passage contains a number of underlined words. These words may not be familiar to you, but you can figure them out.

1. Work with a partner. Reread the passage carefully. Look for clues to the meaning of the underlined words. Fill out the following chart with the meaning of the underlined words and the clues that help you find their meaning.

Word	Best Clues	Meaning
production		
auditions		
professional		
distinguished		

Word	Best Clues	Meaning
performance		
profitable		
outstanding		

On Your Own

Real World Connection

When you read an unknown word, reread its sentence to look for clues to its meaning. Then, reread the sentences that surround its sentence for clues. Think about how nearby words and phrases relate to the unknown word. Connect the ideas to come up with a definition for the word.

   Example: When they reached the steep **embankment** by the river, they didn't know how they could climb down it. After some thought, the boy suggested they tie a rope to a tree on top and hold on as they slid down the steep slope.

Find the Best Clues: "steep"; "by the river"; "climb down"; "slope"

Connect the Ideas: The words *steep, climb down,* and *slope* tell me an embankment is a raised wall of earth. *By the river* tells me it holds back water. The word *embankment* contains the root word *bank*, but *bank* has many meanings: "place to keep money," "sloping land leading a river or lake," "long pile or heap," or "to tilt an aircraft in flight.," to name a few. The meanings that make the most sense here is "sloping land leading a river or lake." and "long pile or heap." The words *steep, climb down,* and *by the river* suggest that an *embankment* is a raised wall of earth that holds back the water of a river.

Try these examples yourself.

1 The **impolite** child never said "please" or "thank you" and always took the most comfortable seat.

   Find the Best Clues: _____

   _____

   Connect the Ideas: _____

   _____

2 Her **enthusiasm**, or excitement, showed as she loudly cheered for the team.

Find the Best Clues: _____

Connect the Ideas: _____

3 The **orchestra** walked onstage. The flute players sat in the front, the trumpet players sat in the middle, and the drummers were behind them all.

Find the Best Clues: _____

Connect the Ideas: _____

_____

4 The waiter made an adjustment to the bill to correct his mistake in addition.

What does *adjustment* mean?

A an addition

B a change

C a mistake

D an amount owed

5 Joey was so determined to win the race that he didn't give up when it seemed hopeless.

Which is the best clue to the meaning of *determined*?

A was so

B win the race

C didn't give up

D it seemed hopeless

6 When Pam asked for the athlete's signature, he took a pen and wrote his name on the ball.

Which words give the best clue to the meaning of *signature*? What does *signature* mean?

_____

7 Marisa rummaged through her desk, trying to find a pen that worked.

What does *rummaged* mean?

_____

Measuring Up® to the New York Common Core

8 Read these sentences.

> **The vegetation supported the animals through the winter. The acorns from the oak trees, the fallen apples, and the berries from the bushes were great meals for squirrels and deer.**

On your own sheet of paper, write the clues that help you figure out the meaning of *vegetation*. Explain how you connected the clues to the meaning of the word. Then write a second paragraph like the one above. Challenge a partner to find clues to the meaning of an important word in your passage.

RF.4.4	Read with sufficient accuracy and fluency to support comprehension. **a.** Read on-level text with purpose and understanding.
SL.4.1	Engage effectively in a range of collaborative discussions with diverse partners on grade 4 topics and texts, building on others' ideas and expressing their own clearly.
SL.4.3	Identify the reasons and evidence a speaker provides to support particular points.
L.4.6	Acquire and use accurately grade-appropriate general academic and domain-specific words and phrases, including those that signal precise actions, emotions, or states of being and that are basic to a particular topic.
CCR.L.3	Apply knowledge of language to understand how language functions in different contexts, to make effective choices for meaning or style, and to comprehend more fully when reading or listening.
CCR.L.6	Acquire and use accurately a range of general academic and domain-specific words and phrases sufficient for reading, writing, speaking, and listening at the college and career readiness level; demonstrate independence in gathering vocabulary knowledge when encountering an unknown term important to comprehension or expression.
CRR.R.10	Read and comprehend complex literary and informational texts independently and proficiently.

Understand the Standards

Multicultural Connection

Imagine you want to learn about life in another country. How can you find out what it is like? You can read about it—in books, in magazines, or on the Internet. Understanding what you read allows you to learn and share your new information.

> **Words to Know**
> purpose
> summary
> draw conclusions

Follow these guidelines to understand your reading:

- **Set a purpose.** Your **purpose**, or reason for reading, and the text are connected. You read stories for enjoyment and informational texts to learn.

- **Check your understanding.** As you read, stop occasionally to check your understanding. Ask and answer questions, make predictions and connections, and review the main ideas or events you have read so far. Reread to clear up confusion. Write a **summary**, a brief statement of the text's main ideas.

- **Form ideas and opinions.** Think about the text and your reactions to it. Use details from the text to **draw conclusions** about the author, the characters, or the topic. Use details from the text to support your claims and opinions.

- **Discuss.** Share your ideas about the text and the support for those ideas. Listen to others' ideas and support. Discuss the ways your ideas are the same and different.

Guided Instruction

Before you begin, set a purpose for reading. To improve understanding, take time to ask and answer questions, make predictions and connections, and summarize. Use the information you gather to form ideas and opinions.

Science Connection

A Big Change in Photography

Not long ago, taking a picture required you to buy film. That limited the number of pictures you could take to 36. When you took the picture, you had no idea what it looked like until you took the film to the store to be developed. With the invention of digital photography, all of that changed. Now you can take hundreds of pictures without film. You can view pictures immediately to make sure they are good. You can print only the photos you like, saving money and paper. The transformation from film to digital has made photography an accessible, inexpensive hobby for all to enjoy.

Guided Questions

What prediction about content can you make from reading just the title?

_____

_____

_____

Is the writer in favor of or against digital photography? What makes you draw this conclusion?

_____

_____

_____

Complete the following activities based on the passage you just read.

1. What purpose did you set for reading this text? How is your purpose connected to the text?

_____

_____

2. Which words show how the author feels about digital photography?

_____

_____

3. What is the main idea of the text? State it in your own words.

_____

_____

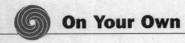 **On Your Own**

Read the passage, then complete the activities that follow.

A Dangerous Job

When you hear someone say, "Let's go fishing," you probably think of a relaxing day spent by a lake. Many people fish for recreation, but commercial fishing is a dangerous job. How far and how long commercial fishermen and -women travel depends on the kind of fish they want to catch. Some boats go out for a day, and others go for a month. While at sea, the workers have to set lines or traps for the fish. When they come back, they haul hundreds of pounds of fish onboard. When the weather is bad, the work becomes even scarier. These jobs are so thrilling that several television shows feature stories about them.

Complete the following activities based on the passage you just read.

1 Reread the passage and record your reading process in the chart. Discuss your ideas with a partner.

Set a purpose. What is your purpose for reading this passage? How does it connect with the kind of text?	
Check your understanding. What questions did you ask? What is the main idea of the passage?	
Form Ideas and Opinions. Which words tell how the author feels about fishing as a job?	
Discuss. Discuss your ideas and share the reasons and evidence you found in the text. Then listen to your partner. What support does he or she give for ideas and opinions?	

Measuring Up® to the New York Common Core

2 The most likely purpose for reading informational texts is

    A to learn about something.

    B to be convinced.

    C to enjoy a story.

    D to read a description.

3 Which question is not answered in the passage?

    A How are fishing for fun and fishing for a job different?

    B How long do fishing boats stay at sea?

    C What kinds of fish do the workers fish for?

    D Why do television shows feature stories about fishing?

4 What questions did you ask as you read the passage?

_____

_____

_____

5 What connections can you make to this passage? In other words, what ideas or information does this passage remind you of?

_____

_____

_____

 6 On your own sheet of paper, write an opinion or idea about the passage. Then explain why you feel the way you do. Be sure to use support from the passage for your ideas. Then compare your responses with the responses of a small group of classmates. Explore where and why you agree and disagree. Come to a consensus.

Explore the many purposes for reading through the following activity.

Critical Thinking

7   In a small group, brainstorm to list all the things you read in the past day. Be as complete as you can. Include school books and magazines, TV listings, the backs of cereal boxes, street signs, warning signs at construction sites, notes on the refrigerator door, and everything else. Then group these reading materials into categories. Base your categories on your purpose for reading the specific item. Then work together to create a One Day of Reading mural. Illustrate it with drawings, photographs, and examples of text. Display it outside your classroom.

Reading Aloud

RF.4.4	Read with sufficient accuracy and fluency to support comprehension. **b.** Read on-level prose and poetry orally with accuracy, appropriate rate, and expression on successive readings.
SL.4.1	Engage effectively in a range of collaborative discussions with diverse partners on grade 4 topics and texts, building on others' ideas and expressing their own clearly.

 Understand the Standards

Imagine reading aloud in class. You come across this paragraph:

> "Oh, Mom," Ty whined, "do I *have* to dry those dishes?" He anticipated the worst, but he thought he would ask.

Words to Know
fluent
rate
pronounce
expression

How would you use your voice to capture the feeling of Ty's words? How would you read the word *have*? What would you do if you didn't know how to pronounce *anticipated*?

Readers who are **fluent** read aloud smoothly and easily, letting words flow together to make sentences. To be a fluent reader, follow these guidelines:

- Don't read too quickly and don't pause after each word. Instead, choose an appropriate **rate**, or speed. Sometimes you will need to slow down for difficult passages. Other times you will speed up to show the feeling of the text.

- Take the time to sound out unfamiliar words and **pronounce**, or say, them properly. Link letters to sounds and use what you know about saying other words to help you pronounce new words correctly.

- Read with **expression**, showing the feeling of the text or the character with your voice. Look for words like *whined* in the above example for clues to how to read.

- Practice as often as possible. The more you read aloud, the more smoothly and easily you will be able to read.

Guided Instruction

Prepare to read this text aloud. Skim it to find words that you don't know and sound them out. Look for clues that tell how to read characters' words. Think about the feeling of the story that you will express with your voice.

The Mystery of the Old House

Kelly and Abe were playing at the park. They realized it was getting dark, so they decided to head home immediately. As they walked past the old abandoned house on the corner, Kelly heard a squeak. She jumped when she saw the door swing back and forth. "Abe," she said with fear seeping through her voice, "did you see that?"

What groups of words need to be kept together when you read aloud?

_____

_____

_____

What in the story do you want to use your voice to build up to?

_____

_____

_____

Answer these questions about reading the text aloud.

1. Which words did you need to sound out?

_____

2. Which words give clues about how to read Kelly's words?

_____

3. What is the feeling of this text? How can you read to show this feeling?

_____

_____

_____

Collaborative Learning

4. Take turns reading the text aloud with a partner. Read it at least two times each. How does the reading change the second time?

_____

On Your Own

Prepare to read the passage aloud. Then take turns reading aloud with a partner.

It was a cold, snowy night. Peter groaned as he put on his coat to take his new puppy outside. He wasn't paying attention. Then he suddenly realized she wasn't hooked to the leash he held.

"Sadie! Sadie! Come here immediately!" Peter bellowed. His puppy had escaped, and he was in a panic. "Sadie, where are you?!" he screeched as he sprinted through the snow desperately searching.

Within seconds, Sadie came barreling toward the boy from a neighbor's backyard. "Oh, Sadie, I was *so* worried," he said with delight as his puppy licked his face and wagged her tail.

Answer and discuss the questions below.

1 How did you read Peter's words in the second paragraph? Which words tell you how to read his dialogue?

_____

_____

2 How did you adjust, or change, your reading rate through the text?

_____

_____

_____

3 What feelings did you try to express with your reading? How did you express them?

_____

_____

_____

4 Which word has the same sound as the *ow* in *bellowed*?

   A groaned

   B outside

   C you

   D neighbor's

5 If the dog is barreling, it is

   A shaped like a barrel.

   B rolling down a hill.

   C going a different direction.

   D moving really quickly.

6 Imagine you don't know how to pronounce the word *desperately*. How would you break it down to sound it out?

_____

_____

_____

7 How did you read Peter's words in the last paragraph? What clues told you how to read his words?

_____

_____

Elevate **8** Imagine you are directing a play of this story. Work with two classmates to divide the passage into speaking parts. Then agree on instructions for the narrator and Peter. Use clues from the text to tell each classmate how to read his or her lines.

Kick It Up

Chapter 1

Spell Tricky Words

Collaborative Learning

Have you heard that you can spell *fish* this way: *ghoti*? Take the *gh* from *rough,* add the *o* from *women,* and finish with the *ti* from *nation. Ghoti = fish*! English is not easy! Many letters have multiple sounds.

Work with a small group. Brainstorm multiple ways to spell *fish,* or choose a word of your own. Some examples are given here.

Make sure that you can support your respellings with phonics rules and examples.

Once you have a good list, decide on a way to display your list on the bulletin board. Use art supplies, old magazines, or pictures you download and print.

Investigate Word Origins

Language Connection

Choose a partner to help investigate this question. Find a book that you both like. Each of you can choose a paragraph from the book. Make a chart that looks like this:

| Word | Greek or Latin? |

Use the chart and a print or online dictionary. Tell whether each word in the paragraph you chose comes from Greek or Latin. Out of the total words in your paragraph, how many came from Greek or Latin? Express it as a percent, if you know how. Tell your classmates what you discovered. What does that tell you about the English language?

Compare the Reading of Fiction and Nonfiction

Collaborative Learning

Work with some classmates. Visit the library to choose two books. Make sure that they are both at your grade level, and that one is fiction and is one nonfiction. Now design an experiment that answers these questions.

- Can I read nonfiction as fast as I read fiction?

- Can I answer questions about my reading as easily when I'm reading nonfiction as when I'm reading fiction?

- What changes do I make in my reading when I read nonfiction instead of fiction? Why do I change the way I read?

Work together to find a way to record your findings. Would a chart or graph help you explain what you learned? Then report your findings to the class.

Read for Different Audiences

Music/Arts Connection

Choose two groups of people in your school. For example, you might choose a group of kindergartners and a group of parent volunteers. Work with some friends to choose one poem to read aloud to both groups. Think about these questions.

- What kind of poem would work for both groups? Why?

- Will we change the way we read from one group to the other? How?

- How do we expect each audience to react to our reading?

Perform the reading. If you can, have one friend videotape the reading. Afterward, watch the video. Did things turn out the way you expected? Did you choose the right poem for your audiences? How would you do things differently next time?

Lesson 6

Multiple-Meaning Words

L.4.4	Determine or clarify the meaning of unknown and multiple-meaning words and phrases based on grade 4 reading and content, choosing flexibly from a range of strategies.
L.4.6	Acquire and use accurately grade-appropriate general academic and domain-specific words and phrases, including those that signal precise actions, emotions, or states of being and that are basic to a particular topic.
CCR.L.3	Apply knowledge of language to understand how language functions in different contexts, to make effective choices for meaning or style, and to comprehend more fully when reading or listening.
CCR.L.4	Determine or clarify the meaning of multiple-meaning words and phrases by using context clues, analyzing meaningful word parts, and consulting general and specialized reference materials, as appropriate.
CCR.L.6	Acquire and use accurately a range of general academic and domain-specific words and phrases sufficient for reading, writing, speaking, and listening at the college and career readiness level; demonstrate independence in gathering vocabulary knowledge when encountering an unknown term important to comprehension or expression.

Understand the Standards

Imagine that you are reading a story for class. You come across this sentence:

> The detective saw a light coming from the second story of the house, so she knocked on the door to see if anyone was home.

Words to Know

multiple-meaning words
context clues
dictionary

This sentence has two words with more than one meaning: *light* and *story*.

○ **Multiple-meaning words** have more than one meaning, depending on how they are used in a sentence.

Sometimes the same word is used as different parts of speech. For example, a word might be a noun and a verb. When you come across a sentence with a multiple-meaning word, you can use several strategies to figure out what the word means in that sentence.

1. You can look for **context clues**, other words or phrases that hint at the meaning.

2. You can use a **dictionary**, which will give you all the different meanings of a word.

3. You can replace the multiple-meaning word with different definitions until you find the one that makes sense in the sentence.

The word *light* can mean "to begin to burn," "to brighten," "pale," or "a glow."

The word *story* can mean "tale" or "floor or level of a building."

In the sentence above, the detective sees a light. *Light* is a noun in this sentence. Look at the meanings above and place each one of them in the sentence. The one that makes sense is "a glow."

The light comes from the second story of a house. In this sentence, *story* does not mean a tale. The word *house* is a clue that the meaning is "floor or level of a building."

☉ Guided Instruction

Read the passage. Pay particular attention to the underlined multiple-meaning words.

 A Perfect Part

Mrs. Rodriguez, the <u>drama</u> instructor, took <u>roll</u> and then put down her <u>pen</u>, stood up from her desk, and began to <u>address</u> the class.

"As you know, today is the first day of auditions for the fourth-grade <u>play</u>. Since this play requires a large <u>cast</u>, we want everyone to participate. It doesn't matter if you have extensive experience or none at all, we can find a role for you."

Pedro raised his hand. "Are there any invisible <u>parts</u>?" asked Pedro. "I'm a musician. I don't want to appear in a school play!"

Mrs. Rodriguez smiled. "Actually, Pedro," responded Mrs. Rodriguez, grinning mischievously. "I have the perfect role for you, Mr. Invisible. I think you're going to have a blast!"

Pedro looked confused until he talked to Mrs. Rodriguez by himself in another classroom. He returned with the most enormous grin on his face. The other children auditioned, were given roles that best <u>fit</u> their personality, and spent hours learning their <u>lines</u>. Everyone speculated about what role Pedro had been given. Mrs. Rodriguez said it was a surprise. Some of the kids tried to <u>fish</u> for information, but neither Pedro nor the drama teacher would reveal their secret.

On the night of the show, the curtains rose, revealing an empty stage. And then, out of the silence, came the sweet sounds of Pedro's voice. He sat offstage, singing a long tune about the play

Guided Questions

The word *roll* has multiple meanings. What does the *roll* mean as a noun?

_____

_____

_____

_____

_____

_____

_____

_____

_____

As a verb?

_____

_____

_____

How do you figure out which meaning fits the sentence in the first paragraph?

_____

_____

_____

_____

_____

 Measuring Up® to the New York Common Core

while strumming his guitar. When the song ended, the audience roared, and Pedro, who had wanted to be invisible, ran onto the stage and made a <u>bow</u>. It was an extraordinary beginning to the play, an experience Pedro would never forget.

Guided Questions

Complete these activities based on the passage you just read.

1. Work with a partner to fill in the following chart. Use a dictionary to help you write two meanings for each multiple-meaning word. Then put a star by the meaning that fits the context of "A Perfect Part."

Word	Meaning 1	Meaning 2
drama		
pen		
address		
play		
cast		
parts		
fit		
lines		
fish		
bow		

2. There are multiple-meaning words in the passage that are not underlined. Identify one such word. Give at least two of its meanings, then explain what it means in "A Perfect Part."

_____

_____

_____

_____

_____

_____

_____

On Your Own

You will often come across multiple-meaning words when you read. You can use context clues and, if needed, a dictionary to figure out which meaning is correct for the sentence.

Example: The angry boss said she would <u>fire</u> the cook if she was late to work again.

The dictionary says that *fire* can be a verb that means "to let go of a worker" or a noun that means "flame." The clues *boss* and *work* tell you that in this context *fire* means "to let go of a worker."

Use a dictionary to write two possible definitions for each underlined word. Then, use context clues to tell which definition fits.

1 The movie was two hours <u>long</u>.

Think: _____

_____

_____

2 Sally <u>pet</u> her cat Henry and then let him out for the night.

Think: _____

_____

3 The nurse will <u>dress</u> the wound on the boy's knee to keep it protected.

Think: _____

Complete the following activities on multiple-meaning words.

4 How does a dictionary identify the different meanings of a word?

_____

5 What does *post* mean in the following sentence?

She will <u>post</u> the letter today so it arrives by Monday.

A announce

B pole

C job

D send

6 Which sentence has the same meaning of *light* as in the following sentence?

His new phone is <u>light</u> as a feather.

A He has light skin, so he should use extra sunblock.

B I turned on a light in the room.

C I just ate a light dinner.

D The suitcase is light, so I won't need help carrying it.

7 Think of two meanings for the word *hit*. Write two different sentences using the word in different ways.

_____

_____

8 What does the multiple-meaning word *stop* mean in the following sentence?

Please <u>stop</u> using my pens.

_____

_____

 9 Explain three ways you can figure out the definition of an unfamiliar multiple-meaning word.

Similes and Metaphors

L.4.5   Demonstrate understanding of figurative language, word relationships, and nuances in word meanings.
a. Explain the meaning of simple similes and metaphors in context.

CCR.L.5   Demonstrate understanding of figurative language, word relationships, and nuances in word meanings.

Understand the Standards

As you read a description, you come across the following sentences.

> The snow was a white blanket across the once-green field. Louise ran like the wind to get her sled and tell her friends to join her for a ride.

Words to Know
metaphor
simile

Literature Connection

The sentences use a metaphor and a simile. Metaphors and similes help readers imagine what the writer is describing.

- A **metaphor** compares two things:

  The snow was a white blanket.

- A **simile** compares two things using the word *like* or *as*:

  Louise ran like the wind.

When you see a metaphor or a smile, ask yourself, "What might the things being compared have in common?"

In the metaphor, snow is compared to a white blanket. Snow and a white blanket are the same color (white) and they both cover things. The snow covers the earth, while a blanket covers a bed.

In the simile, the writer describes how the narrator runs. She compares the narrator's running to the wind. The wind blows very fast, so the writer is saying that Louise ran fast.

Guided Instruction

You can understand the meaning of metaphors and similes better if you stop to think about them. First, identify what two things are being compared. Then think about how the two things might be alike. You can also test your understanding of literary terms and identify whether the comparison is a simile or a metaphor. In general, similes are much more common than metaphors.

Example: I can carry my kitten everywhere; she is a feather.

Think: Since a kitten is not a feather, this must be a metaphor. To understand what the writer means, I need to identify what's being compared and how these two thing might be alike:

What is being compared: a kitten and a feather

How they might be alike: Both the kitten and the feather are soft, and they might be the same color. However, the writer talks about carrying the kitten everywhere. This means the kitten is easy to carry, probably because she doesn't weigh much. In other words, the writer thinks the kitten is as light as a feather.

Meaning: The kitten is light in weight; the kitten is easy to carry.

Simile or metaphor? *(circle one)*

Now try it yourself. What do these sentences mean?

1. **My brother's bedroom was as smelly as a skunk.**

    What is being compared: _____

    How they might be alike: _____

    Meaning: _____

    Simile or metaphor?

2. **Wendy is the most thoughtful person I know. She is a true gem.**

    What is being compared: _____

    How they might be alike: _____

    Meaning: _____

    Simile or metaphor?

3. That dancer is as pretty as a picture.

What is being compared: _____

How they might be alike: _____

Meaning: _____

Simile or metaphor?

4. Ask Maria—she's a regular encyclopedia.

What is being compared: _____

How they might be alike: _____

Meaning: _____

Simile or metaphor?

On Your Own

In a small group, read each sentence. Then tell what is being compared, whether the comparison is a simile or a metaphor, and how the two things are alike.

Example

The old man's skin was as tough as leather.

Explain: The man's skin is being compared to leather. This is a simile. Both leather and the man's skin are tough.

Try these examples yourself.

1 The little girl is as delicate as a flower.

Explain: _____

_____

2 My grandma is a sturdy oak tree.

Explain: _____

_____

 Measuring Up® to the New York Common Core

3 **The football player was as big as a bus.**

Explain: _____

_____

4 If you want to tell that something smelled good, you might compare the smell to

A a rose.

B a pig.

C a garbage bin.

D a rotten egg.

5 "He ran like a race car" means he ran

A clumsily.

B loudly.

C backward.

D fast.

6 Explain the simile "The child ate like a bird."

_____

_____

7 If people told you that you and your best friend were "two peas in a pod," what would they mean? Explain.

_____

_____

 8 Read this passage. Then, on your own sheet of paper, write your answer to the question.

> **The audience waited for the play to start. Backstage, the helpers were busy bees. They got the set ready and helped the actors get dressed.**

Tell what is compared. Evaluate the metaphor. How does the comparison help you imagine the scene? Then work with a partner. Imagine what the theater, the sets, the costumes, and the actors looked like. Create a list of five metaphors and five similes to describe what you see in your minds.

L.4.5	Demonstrate understanding of figurative language, word relationships, and nuances in word meanings. **b.** Recognize and explain the meaning of common idioms, adages, and proverbs.
L.4.6	Acquire and use accurately grade-appropriate general academic and domain-specific words and phrases, including those that signal precise actions, emotions, or states of being and that are basic to a particular topic.
SL.4.1	Engage effectively in a range of collaborative discussions with diverse partners on grade 4 topics and texts, building on others' ideas and expressing their own clearly.
CCR.L.3	Apply knowledge of language to understand how language functions in different contexts, to make effective choices for meaning or style, and to comprehend more fully when reading or listening.
CCR.L.5	Demonstrate understanding of figurative language word relationships, and nuances in word meanings.
CCR.L.6	Acquire and use accurately a range of general academic and domain-specific words and phrases sufficient for reading, writing, speaking, and listening at the college and career readiness level; demonstrate independence in gathering vocabulary knowledge when encountering an unknown term important to comprehension or expression.
CCR.SL.1	Prepare for and participate effectively in a range of conversations and collaborations with diverse partners, building on others' ideas and expressing their own clearly and persuasively.

Understand the Standards

Imagine that you are reading a novel for class. You come across this paragraph:

> After the game was called off, Dennis found himself stuck sitting beside the cooler. "Waste not, want not," he said, helping himself to the team's water and snacks.

Words to Know
idiom
adage
proverb
context clues

Many parts of this simple paragraph would be difficult for a reader who was new to English. That is because it contains words that are used in unusual ways.

Did someone telephone about the game? Is that why it was "called off"? Was Dennis lost? If not, how did he "find himself"? Did Dennis sit in something sticky? Is that why he was "stuck sitting beside the cooler"? Finally, what did Dennis mean when he said, "Waste not, want not"?

Writers use words in ways that are not always literal. Understanding idioms and adages can help you read and listen with better understanding.

○ An **idiom** is any phrase whose meaning cannot be inferred from the words in the phrase.

   called off = "canceled" or "postponed"

   found himself = "discovered that he was"

   stuck sitting = "forced to sit"

○ An **adage** is an old saying or **proverb**, often one that passes along wisdom.

   Waste not, want not = "If you take advantage of this, you will not be in need."

Guided Instruction

Read the passage. Talk about the underlined idioms and adages. What does each one mean?

Health Connection

Food for Thought

By the time the bus returned to the school, the cooler was empty. Dennis was feeling a bit <u>under the weather</u>.

"Ugh," he said, clutching his stomach. "I should have remembered what my grandmother always said: '<u>Eat to live, not live to eat.</u>'"

His teammates saw the empty cooler and <u>blew up</u> at Dennis.

"I knew we should have <u>kept our eye on him</u>," said Bruno.

"From now on, the cooler is <u>off limits</u> to Dennis," growled Scott.

"<u>Give him a break</u>," said Coach Rodriguez, looking at Dennis's unhappy face. "Hey, <u>when one door shuts, another opens</u>. I'll take you all out to lunch."

"<u>Count me out</u>," groaned Dennis. "I'll have to <u>take a rain check</u>. I've really learned my lesson, though."

"<u>Better late than never</u>!" said the coach cheerfully.

Guided Questions

What happens in the passage?

_____

_____

_____

_____

_____

Is it easy to understand the passage? Why or why not?

_____

_____

_____

_____

Which are a bigger barrier to understanding: idioms or adages?

_____

_____

_____

_____

Complete the following chart based on the passage you just read.

Critical Thinking

1. Work with a partner. Identify the idioms and adages in the passage. Fill in the first column of the two tables. Be sure to list the idioms in the top table and the adages in the bottom table. Discuss what the idioms and adages mean. When you agree on a meaning, fill in the appropriate box in the chart. Be prepared to explain and defend your responses.

Idiom	Meaning

Adage	Meaning

On Your Own

Native English speakers learn many, many idioms and adages over the course of a lifetime. Despite this, you will often come across idioms and adages you do not know. You can use **context clues** and what you already know to figure out their meaning.

Example: The workers cut corners while paving the highway. After just a few months, there were many new potholes.

First, think about what words do not seem to be used with their literal meanings. The phrase. In this example, "cut corners" does not make sense when taken literally. Why would carving angles cause potholes? "Cut corners" must be an idiom. You can determine what this idiom means by looking for context clues. If there were new potholes after just a few months, the workers didn't do a good job. They did fast, cheap work. That's what "cut corners" must mean.

Read each sentence. Determine what words are not being used literally. Then explain the sentence means on the lines provided.

1 After Liv and Bridget didn't speak to each other for a week, Liv's mom suggested that they should try to clear the air with a quiet conversation.

_____

_____

2 Although Stuart is a good piano player, he can't hold a candle to his uncle, who plays for a living with the Philharmonic Orchestra.

_____

_____

3 Surprised to find that the oddly dressed new classmate was smart and funny, Becky reminded herself that she should never judge a book by its cover.

_____

_____

_____

Complete the following exercises.

4 If your homework were easy, you might call it

   A a toss-up.

   B a shot in the dark.

   C a dime a dozen.

   D a piece of cake.

5 Read the sentence below.

   He who hesitates is lost.

Which is the best rewording of this adage?

   A Don't slow down when you are lost.

   B If you take too long, you may miss a chance.

   C A person who is aimless is likely to dawdle.

   D Find yourself without delay.

6   What does it mean to feel "on top of the world"?

_____

7   Read the adage below.

Many hands make light work.

In your own words, tell what this means.

_____

8   When you don't want to do something, you might say that you are "dragging your feet." On your own sheet of paper, explain why this idiom is a good, descriptive use of figurative language. Then, with a partner, collect and display photos, videos, and drawings that show the real meaning of "dragging your feet." Be ready to explain and defend your choices.

Critical Thinking

9   Work with a partner. Find a collection of adages online or in the library. They can be serious or humorous. Choose one that you think is especially appropriate for people your age. Then create a multimedia display that helps explain its meaning. Include music, photographs, and a story you write that uses that adage as its last line. If you wish, you may put a humorous spin on a traditional adage. Present your multimedia project to classmates.

L.4.5	Demonstrate understanding of figurative language, word relationships, and nuances in word meanings.
	c. Demonstrate understanding of words by relating them to their opposites and to words with similar but not identical meanings.
CCR.L.5	Demonstrate understanding of figurative language, word relationships, and nuances in word meanings.

 ## Understand the Standards

Imagine that one day you're reading while your friend does a crossword puzzle. She says to you, "What's a three-letter word that means *miserable*?" "*Sad*!" you respond. You've just given your friend a synonym for *miserable* and helped her solve a clue in her crossword puzzle.

> **Words to Know**
> synonyms
> antonyms

- **Synonyms** are words that have similar (close) but not identical (exactly the same) meanings.

    Sad and *miserable* are synonyms.

If your friend had asked you for a word that meant the opposite of *miserable*, you might have said *happy*. *Happy* is an antonym for *miserable*.

- **Antonyms** are words that have the opposite meaning.

    Happy and *miserable* are antonyms.

You can find synonyms and antonyms by using a dictionary or a thesaurus. You can also think of words you already know.

Guided Instruction

One way to remember synonyms and antonyms is by "plugging in" other words. When you swap a word in a sentence with its synonym, the new sentence will mean about the same thing as the old sentence. When you swap a word with its antonym, the new sentence will mean the opposite of the old sentence.

In the following exercises, think about what each word choice means. When you choose a synonym, choose the word that is closest in meaning to the underlined word. When you choose an antonym, choose the word that is most nearly the opposite of the underlined word.

Example: He is a <u>generous</u> person.

Synonym: (giving)　　　　nervous　　　　brave

Antonym: fearful　　　　(stingy)　　　　friendly

1. Raquel has been my <u>friend</u> since first grade.

   Synonym: teacher　　　　pal　　　　stranger

   Antonym: enemy　　　　sister　　　　classmate

2. My bedroom was <u>messy</u>.

   Synonym: wrong　　　　untidy　　　　orderly

   Antonym: neat　　　　colorful　　　　dirty

3. Pete was nearly always <u>absent</u>.

   Synonym: bored　　　　silly　　　　gone

   Antonym: present　　　　happy　　　　angry

On Your Own

Discuss

In a small group, read each sentence. Then, follow the instructions to correctly rewrite the sentences. Use a dictionary or thesaurus if necessary.

Example: I <u>accept</u> your apology.

Rewrite the sentence using an antonym:

I <u>reject</u> your apology.

1 She was <u>astonished</u> by her friends' foolish act.

Rewrite the sentence using a synonym:

_____

2 The road was too <u>narrow</u>.

Rewrite the sentence using an antonym:

_____

3 His shoe was <u>enormous</u>.

   a. Rewrite the sentence using an antonym:

   _____

   b. Rewrite the sentence using a synonym:

_____

4 At 2 o'clock, she was <u>awake</u>.

   a. Rewrite the sentence using an antonym:

_____

   b. Rewrite the sentence using a synonym:

_____

Complete the following activities.

5 An antonym of *dangerous* is

A desperate.

B scary.

C safe.

D mad.

6 A synonym for *soothe* is

A hurt.

B anger.

C soft.

D calm.

7 *Cried* is a synonym for *sobbed*. How are the two words slightly different in meaning?

_____

8 Fill in the following sentence with a word and then with an antonym for that word. Explain how the meaning of the sentence changes.

I found the movie _____.

_____

_____

_____

 9 Read this passage.

Television viewers were upset by the news. However, the people involved were even more distraught.

What are the two synonyms in this passage? How does knowing these words are synonyms help you understand the meaning of the passage? Rewrite the passage. Replace the synonyms you found with their antonyms. Next, write a pair of sentences that have words in them that you can replace with their antonyms. Share your sentences with the class.

Lesson 10

Reference Materials

L.4.4	Determine or clarify the meaning of unknown and multiple-meaning words and phrases based on grade 4 reading and content, choosing flexibly from a range of strategies.
	c. Consult reference materials, both print and digital, to find the pronunciation and determine or clarify the precise meaning of words and phrases.
L.4.6	Acquire and use accurately grade-appropriate general academic and domain-specific words and phrases, including those that signal precise actions, emotions, or states of being and that are basic to a particular topic.
CCR.L.3	Apply knowledge of language to understand how language functions in different contexts, to make effective choices for meaning or style, and to comprehend more fully when reading or listening.
CCR.L.4	Determine or clarify the meaning of unknown and multiple-meaning words and phrases by using context clues, analyzing meaningful word parts, and consulting general and specialized reference materials, as appropriate.
CCR.L.6	Acquire and use accurately a range of general academic and domain-specific words and phrases sufficient for reading, writing, speaking, and listening at the college and career readiness level; demonstrate independence in gathering vocabulary knowledge when encountering an unknown term important to comprehension or expression.

Understand the Standards

Sometimes when you are reading, you will come across words you do not know.

> First, we bought soil and seeds for the nursery.

Words to Know
reference material
dictionary
glossary
thesaurus

You know one meaning of *nursery* is a child's room, but this meaning does not make sense in this sentence. You decide *nursery* is a multiple-meaning word. You will choose the best **reference material** to look up the word. Here are some reference materials. They are all organized alphabetically.

- A **dictionary** tells you how to pronounce a word and what it means.

- A **glossary** is a list at the end of a book that defines important words in the book.

- A **thesaurus** has both definitions and synonyms, words with similar meanings.

Since the book you are reading has no glossary, you decide to look up the word in the dictionary:

part of speech   pronunciation   definition

nursery *noun* \nərs-sə-rē\ 1. a child's bedroom 2. a place where plants are grown 3. a place where animals grow or are cared for

The entry has three definitions of *nursery*. Notice that the word is pronounced the same for all three definitions. (Dictionaries include a pronunciation guide, telling you what the pronunciation symbols mean. Some online dictionaries have a recording of the word so you can hear it pronounced.) The first and third meanings do not fit the sentence. The second meaning, "a place where plants are grown," makes the most sense.

Guided Instruction

Language Connection

A dictionary is helpful when you need to find the meaning of a word or determine how a word is pronounced. Read the dictionary entries, then answer the questions that follow them.

> [1]**purse** *n* 1. a bag that holds money
>
> [2]**purse** *v* 1. to contract into a round shape

1. What do the *n* and the *v* in the entries for *purse* tell you?

_____

_____

2. Which meaning of *purse* fits this sentence?

I purse my lips after I drink sour lemonade.

_____

> [1]**address** \ə dres´\ *verb* 1. to give a speech to
>
> [2]**address** \a´dres\ *noun* 1. directions for delivery on an envelope or parcel

3. Is *address* pronounced the same way for both the verb and the noun? How do you know?

_____

_____

_____

4. Which meaning of address fits this sentence?

The principal will address the crowd.

_____

A dictionary and a thesaurus are both helpful when you are looking for exactly the right word. A thesaurus will give you a list of synonyms (and sometimes a few antonyms). You can then look up the synonyms to find the one with the right shade of meaning. A thesaurus also helps you add variety to your words.

Read this thesaurus entry, then complete the activity.

> **excellent** *adjective*
>
> ace, fine, first-rate, splendid, terrific, top

5. Write two or more sentences using at least two of the synonyms for *excellent*. Use a dictionary if you need to.

_____

_____

On Your Own

Complete the following activities.

1 How might you rewrite the following sentence, using synonyms (words with similar meanings) for the underlined words?

The teacher <u>allowed</u> us to swap <u>presents</u> before vacation.

_____

_____

2 **The little girl had a <u>scowl</u> on her face.**

a. Is the *c* in *scowl* pronounced like a *k* or an *s*?

_____

b. What is a synonym for the word *scowl*?

_____

3 The <u>instructor</u> showed us how to <u>operate</u> the machine.

a. What is a synonym for *instructor*?

_____

b. What does the word *operate* mean?

_____

4 In a dictionary, read the definitions for the synonyms *odor* and *stink*. How are definitions similar? How are they different?

_____

5 If you are reading a book with a lot of unknown words, you might look in the back of the book for a

A table of contents.

B thesaurus.

C glossary.

D dictionary.

6 Read the dictionary entry below.

raid \rād\ *noun* a surprise attack

If you knew the ā is a long "a" sound, then you could tell that *raid* rhymes with

A *rid.*

B *fade.*

C *mad.*

D *eye.*

 Measuring Up® to the New York Common Core

Read the dictionary entry below.

> ¹**lead** \lēd\ *noun* 1. a position at the front 2. a main role in a movie or play
>
> ²**lead** \lēd\ *verb* 1. to be first 2. to guide

7 Which meaning of *lead* is correct in this sentence? Explain how you knew.

In the first five minutes of the race, the three runners from our school <u>lead</u> the pack.

_____

_____

8 Write two sentences that use the word *lead* differently. (Do not write the sentence from question 7.)

_____

_____

 9 You are writing about a family trip, and you want to find just the right word to describe a place your family visited. Explain how you can use a thesaurus and then a dictionary to help you. Then write two versions of a short letter on a separate sheet of paper. In the first version, choose words that make the place sound like a perfect place to visit. In the second version, rewrite it with antonyms, or opposites. Make the place sound like a dreadful place to visit.

Play a Word Game

Collaborative Learning

Make a multiple-meaning word game. On 5" × 7" note cards, write clues about multiple-meaning words, either ones you've learned in this chapter or ones you already know. Look out for multiple-meaning words in other classes and in your own reading.

Write two clues for each word, like these for the word *pound*: "a place where stray animals go" or "to hit with a hammer." Use reference materials to help you.

Once everyone in the class has gathered five cards, you can play a game. Make a team with four partners and tell your clues to another team of four. The team that correctly defines more multiple-meaning words wins.

Illustrate a Simile

Media Connection

Similes help writers describe and readers imagine. Work with four of your classmates to make a simile poster. Each classmate chooses a simile you learned in this chapter to illustrate. Be sure that the similes are written in complete sentences.

Divide a large piece of poster board into four parts. Write your simile at the top of your part. Then, draw or search online for pictures that help you illustrate your simile. Think about how the two things being compared in the simile are alike. For example, if your simile is "She is as pretty as a picture," you might show a pretty person and a picture of something pretty.

Share your simile posters with the rest of the class. Explain how the two things being compared are alike.

Create an Idiom Challenge

Collaborative Learning

Prepare yourself for the idiom challenge! Think of one idiom you have learned in this chapter, or look for an idiom on an online site your teacher has approved. Write the idiom on one side of a 5" × 7" note card and the definition on the other side.

Put your idiom note cards into a box. Form a small group of classmates and listen as your teacher reads each idiom aloud to the class. Raise your hand if you know what the idiom means. The first person who raises his or her hand gets to define the idiom and gets one point. Your teacher will keep track of which team gets the most points. Discuss whether formal or informal language was best for your responses.

Once you've finished the game, your teacher will post the idiom cards on a bulletin board. Look at them occasionally to see which ones you remember.

Construct a Thesaurus

Writing Connection

With a small group of your classmates, make your own thesaurus. Your teacher will give your group a list of important words to know. Write each word at the top of a separate sheet of paper. Then, write one synonym and one antonym for each word and hand the paper to another member of your group. The next person should write another synonym and antonym and keep passing the paper until everyone in the group has added a synonym and an antonym. Use a dictionary or thesaurus to help you.

Once everyone in your group has written on every paper, combine all the entries to make one thesaurus. Make sure you correctly alphabetize each vocabulary word. Then, type or handwrite your complete entries to make a thesaurus. Add illustrations that make the meanings of words clear. Make enough copies for each person in the class.

Lesson 11

Differentiating Genres

RL.4.5	Explain major differences between poems, drama, and prose, and refer to the structural elements of poems and drama when writing or speaking about a text.
RL.4.10	By the end of the year, read and comprehend literature, including stories, dramas, and poetry, in the grades 4–5 text complexity band proficiently, with scaffolding as needed at the high end of the range.
CCR.R.10	Read and comprehend complex literary and informational texts independently and proficiently.
CCR.R.11	Respond to literature by employing knowledge of literary language, textual features, and forms to read and comprehend, reflect upon, and interpret literary texts from a variety of genres and a wide spectrum of American and world cultures.
CCR.SL.1	Prepare for and participate effectively in a range of conversations and collaborations with diverse partners, building on others' ideas and expressing their own clearly and persuasively.

Understand the Standards

Literature Connection

You read many different kinds of writing for class. **Fiction** is writing that comes from a writer's imagination. Among the kinds, or **genres**, of fiction writing you will read are stories, poems, and plays.

> **Words to Know**
> fiction
> genres
> verses
> rhyme
> rhythm
> stage directions
> dialogue

- A story is about events and people that a writer makes up.

    The two teams met each other on the playing field. The faces of the captains were determined. "You don't have a chance!" Amy said, and her team let out a cheer.

- A poem is a work that uses language that appeals to the emotions and creates a mental image. It may include **verses**, or groups of lines; **rhyme**, or sounds that repeat at the end of lines; and **rhythm**, or stresses on certain syllables or words.

    The eagle let out a cry that was harsh
    As it swiftly soared high above the marsh.

- A play is a work meant to be performed for an audience. It has a cast, or a list of the characters that will appear in the play, and includes **stage directions** that tell how the actors move or speak and **dialogue**, the actual words that the actors speak.

    MARTIN: *(pacing nervously)* Where are they? We're going to be late.
    ANDREA: *(soothingly)* Calm down, Martin! We have plenty of time.

Guided Instruction

Read the passage. With a partner, discuss its elements and answer the questions in the margin.

Collaborative Learning

The Twin Prank

Characters:

Jen and Kallie, 10-year-old twins

Sam, their classmate

Meg, their best friend

Jen's bedroom. Meg and the twins sit on the bed, braiding each other's hair.

KALLIE: I am so sick of Sam always playing practical jokes. I think it's time for us to play a joke on him. We haven't pretended to be each other for a long time, Jen.

MEG: Oh, but you've gotten in trouble for doing that! I thought you promised not to do it anymore.

JEN: *(worried)* I don't think we should, Kallie–it always backfires when we do.

KALLIE: *(unconcerned)* We'd be really careful, and nothing bad will happen. Besides, don't you think he deserves it? Remember the goldfish he put in your water glass?

JEN: Oh, that poor fish! It was so awful when I almost drank it! *(shivers)* You're right, he deserves it. So what exactly should we do?

KALLIE: He's my partner in science, so if you take my place, he'll be totally confused when you don't have any idea what we're doing. Just make sure you dress like me on Thursday when we have science lab, and put your hair in a ponytail. He'll figure it out eventually, but we can sure laugh until he does!

Guided Questions

What is the purpose of the list at the beginning of the passage?

_____

_____

Where does this take place? Who is there?

_____

_____

_____

What do Jen and Kallie decide to do? Why do they decide to do this?

_____

_____

_____

_____

_____

Continue working with a partner to complete the following activities about the passage you just read.

1. What genre is this passage? Explain your answer.

_____

_____

2. How do you know how Jen feels about the idea of switching places?

_____

3. In this line, what is the word in parentheses called?

Oh, that poor fish! It was so awful when I almost drank it! *(shivers)*

_____

(Elevate) **4.** How can you tell what the personalities of Kallie, Jen, and Meg are like? Compare the personalities of the three girls. Support your answer with evidence from the passage.

_____

_____

_____

_____

_____

_____

(Elevate) **5.** How is the way you learn about characters in a play different from the way you learn about characters in a story or poem?

_____

_____

_____

_____

6. How would "The Twin Prank" be different if the characters were from a culture that thought pranks were disrespectful?

_____

_____

6. On your own sheet of paper, rewrite "The Twin Prank" as either a poem or a story. Use the elements of the genre you have chosen. Then, in a small group, share and discuss your stories and poems aloud. Revise them based on comments and suggestions from the group.

 On Your Own

When you read fiction, think about what genre you are reading. Look for the elements that identify each kind of fiction.

For each of these exercises, you will read small sections from longer works, then answer questions about them.

1 **Solitary on the beach**
   The boy sat silent on the sand
   As waves lapped gently at his toes
   He felt the water with his hand.

What was your first clue about what kind of text this is?

_____

_____

_____

What kind of text is this? Explain your answer.

_____

_____

2 HANNAH: I think the noise is coming from the attic. It sounds like someone's knocking!

MATTIE: (*fearfully*) Do you think someone's up there?

What kind of text is this? Explain your answer.

_____

_____

3 The boat rocked gently on the lake as Ella cast her fishing line. A moment later, she felt a strong tug. "I think I've caught a fish!" she cried.

What kind of text is this? Explain your answer.

_____

_____

   Measuring Up® to the New York Common Core

RL.4.1	Refer to details and examples in a text when explaining what the text says explicitly and when drawing inferences from the text.
RL.4.11	Recognize, interpret, and make connections in narratives, poetry, and drama to other texts, ideas, cultural perspectives, personal events, and situations.
CCR.R.1	Read closely to determine what the text says explicitly and to make logical inferences from it; cite specific textual evidence when writing or speaking to support conclusions drawn from the text.
CCR.SL.1	Prepare for and participate effectively in a range of conversations and collaborations with diverse partners, building on others' ideas and expressing their own clearly and persuasively.

 ## Understand the Standards

When you read a story for class, you may be asked to remember information, or **details**, about it. The details in a story tell you the answers to the questions *who, what, when, where, why,* and *how.* To recall the details in a selection, ask yourself these questions:

Words to Know
details

○ *Who* is the selection about?

○ *Where* and *when* does the selection take place?

○ *What* happens in the selection?

○ *Why* do the people in the selection act the way they do? *Why* do the events happen?

○ *How* do the events turn out?

○ *How* do people's backgrounds affect what they say and do?

Your answers to these questions can help you understand the selections you read more completely.

Guided Instruction

When you read, look at the details. Think about *who, what, when, where, why,* and *how.*

The New Neighbor

Celia and Raul walked up to the door of the mansion. "I don't think we should do this," Raul said nervously. "I'm sure this place is haunted, and now it's nighttime."

"Mrs. Foster is our new neighbor, and we should welcome her," Celia said, but she was worried, too. She climbed the front steps and rapped on the door, which creaked open slowly, as if it was waiting for them.

"I'm leaving," Raul whispered, and he turned to run.

"Hello, children," a voice said, and suddenly there stood a tiny woman with bright friendly eyes and a warm smile on her face.

Guided Questions

What are the most important words and phrases in the opening paragraph that give details that get you involved in reading the text?

_____

_____

_____

By the end of the passage, what important changes do you notice in the details? Why is this important?

_____

_____

_____

_____

_____

_____

Complete the following activity based on the passage you just read.

1. Fill in the chart with details from the passage.

Who?	What?	When?	Where?	Why?	How?

55

on Language Arts — Level D   Copying is illegal.   Measuring Up® to the New York Common Core

On Your Own

Read the passage. Talk with a partner about the details. Work with a partner to answer the questions.

Science Connection

Lost in the Museum

"This exhibit is so cool," Nate said to Kai as they wandered through the giant heart model. They could see all the veins and arteries, and the sound of a beating heart echoed around them.

"Wait—where is everyone? They were here a minute ago," Kai said, looking around. There was no sign of the rest of the class or of Mr. Sanchez. "Oh no—they're gone, and we're lost!"

The boys dashed frantically around the huge Museum of Science, but there was no sign of their class. "Mr. Sanchez warned us to stay together," Nate reminded his friend, "and he'll be furious if he realizes we're lost!"

"I have an idea," Kai said. "Remember how Mr. Sanchez was talking about the electricity exhibit and how great it was? I'll bet that's where they are!" The boys stopped a guide, who directed them to the electricity exhibit, and there was the class. Mr. Sanchez was giving a talk, so absorbed in his favorite subject that he never noticed as Kai and Nate slipped into place with the others.

Answer the questions based on the passage.

1 Who is this selection about?

_____

2 Where does the selection take place?

_____

3 What happens to the people in the selection? Why does it happen?

_____

_____

4 When does the selection take place?

   A in the summer

   B during a class trip

   C at night

   D after school

5 What do the boys first do when they realize they are lost?

   A They ask for help.

   B They wait where they are.

   C They go home.

   D They run around frantically.

6 What detail about the museum helps to explain why Kai and Nate are lost?

_____

7 How does Kai figure out where the class has gone?

_____

 8 On your own sheet of paper, explain how the boys avoid getting into trouble. Include details from the story. Then work with a partner to extend your understanding of Nate and Kai. Write a paragraph about each that creates a "backstory" for the character that helps you understand the character's behavior in the story. Base your paragraphs on the story. Think about how the cultural backgrounds of the characters might affect each character's behavior.

RL.4.1	Refer to details and examples in a text when explaining what the text says explicitly and when drawing inferences from the text.
CCR.R.1	Read closely to determine what the text says explicitly and to make logical inferences from it; cite specific textual evidence when writing or speaking to support conclusions drawn from the text.
CCR.SL.1	Prepare for and participate effectively in a range of conversations and collaborations with diverse partners, building on others' ideas and expressing their own clearly and persuasively.

 ## Understand the Standards

Imagine that you are reading a story for class. You come across this passage:

> Meg's face grew red and she drew her brows together. She stamped her foot and clenched her fists, trying to stay calm.

Words to Know

inference

The author doesn't tell you exactly how Meg feels, but you can make an **inference** about her feelings. An inference is an intelligent guess. To make an inference, do the following:

- Gather details from the text. The text tells you that Meg's face is red, her fists are clenched, she stamps her feet, and she is having trouble staying calm.

- Think about what you already know. You know that when people are angry, they might behave the way Meg is behaving.

- Use the information to make an intelligent guess. You can infer that Meg is angry.

Writers often will not tell readers everything about a character or an event in a story. Making inferences can help you read between the lines to understand a story more fully.

Guided Instruction

When you read, look at the details. Think about what you already know. Then use that information to make inferences about the characters and the events.

Social Studies Connection

The Social Studies Report

It was Andrew's turn to present his report. As he slowly made his way to the front of the class, his paper trembled in his hand, and when he started to talk, his voice shook.

"Take your time, Andrew," Mr. Wu said gently.

"My report is on the big oil spill and the way it has affected people who fish in the bay," Andrew began. He forced himself to look up at his classmates and saw that they all looked interested, so he took a deep breath and went on.

Guided Questions

How do you feel when you have to stand in the front of the classroom to do something?

_____

_____

What can help you feel more confident up there?

_____

_____

_____

_____

Answer these questions about the passage.

1. What details do you learn about Andrew from the text?

_____

_____

2. What do you already know about people who act like Andrew?

_____

_____

3. What inference can you make about Andrew?

_____

_____

On Your Own

Read the passage. Talk about the details and what you already know. Work with a partner to fill in the chart.

Real World Connection

The Night Prowler

It was very late when Maria woke up. She could hear Sara breathing gently beside her in the tent, but she could hear something else, too—something scratching and tramping beside the tent. Quietly, she poked Sara, trying to wake her up.

"Sara," she hissed, "there's something outside, and I don't know what it is!"

"What—what are you talking about? It's the middle of the night, please let me sleep!" Sara begged. Suddenly there was a crash outside, and both girls sat straight up in their sleeping bags.

"It's going through our backpacks, whatever it is—we must have left some food out there. Give me the flashlight," Maria whispered, "and get ready to run." Sara passed the flashlight to her friend, whimpering softly, and Maria said, "Okay, on the count of three, I'll shine it outside. One, two, three!"

She switched the flashlight on, and through the screen window the girls saw a face peering in at them—a funny little furry face, with mask-like markings on it. The girls screamed, and the face turned away. A minute later, they heard the sound of something running away through the woods.

Details from the text about how the girls feel	What I already know	My inference about how the girls feel

Answer the questions based on the passage.

1   What does the intruder look like?

   A   It has a furry, mask-like face.

   B   It is very large and clumsy.

   C   It looks hungry and fierce.

   D   It looks like a person.

2   What detail tells you that the girls are camping?

   A   They are asleep.

   B   They have a flashlight.

   C   They are in sleeping bags in a tent.

   D   It is nighttime.

3   What do you know about creatures that look like the intruder?

   _____

4   What inference can you make about what the intruder is?

   _____

 5   On your own sheet of paper, make an inference about why the intruder ran away. Include details from the story and your own knowledge to support your inference. Then work with a partner. Decide what kind of intruder you might read about in a different kind of story, maybe a science-fiction story or a history story. Write what could happen.

Lesson 14

Summarizing a Story

RL.4.2	Determine a theme of a story, drama, or poem from details in the text; summarize the text.
CCR.R.2	Determine central ideas or themes of a text and analyze their development; summarize the key supporting details and ideas.
CCR.SL.1	Prepare for and participate effectively in a range of conversations and collaborations with diverse partners, building on others' ideas and expressing their own clearly and persuasively.

 Understand the Standards

Imagine you have just seen a great television show. A friend asks you what it was about. You reply:

Words to Know

summarize

> The show was called "Into the Dark." It was about two scientists who get on a spaceship going to Mars, but something goes wrong. Instead, they find themselves hurtling into outer space. They can't turn the ship around, and they have to decide how they are going to survive.

When a teacher, classmate, or friend wants to know about a story you have just read or a movie you've seen, you don't tell them every single detail of the work. That could take hours! Instead, you **summarize** the work, giving a shorter version of it. When you summarize a story, do the following:

- Give the title of the work.

- Determine the most important events and characters in the story.

- Decide on the most important details in the story. Ask yourself, "Would I understand what happens without this detail?"

- Use your own words to tell what happens in the story, in the order it happens. Your summary should be short.

Summarizing a story can help you remember it and clarify your understanding of it.

Guided Instruction

When you read a story, look at important events, characters, and details.

The Dancing Spider

Ben loved bugs of all kinds, especially spiders. He stopped at every spiderweb he saw to watch the spiders and their activities. One afternoon, he passed an unusually large and beautiful web, and in the center of the web he saw a huge spider. This was not an ordinary spider, though. This spider had shoes on all eight of its legs—dancing shoes!

"I have to tell my science teacher!" Ben cried. Then he thought about what anyone would say if he reported he'd found a spider that wore dancing shoes. "On second thought," he mused, "I think this will be my little secret."

Guided Questions

What is the main idea of this passage? State it as briefly as you can.

_____

_____

_____

_____

What best describes the writer's purpose for writing the story—to entertain or to inform?

_____

_____

Answer the questions about the story.

1. Who is the story about?

   _____

2. What is the most important event that happens in the story?

   _____

3. In your own words, tell what Ben decides to do.

   _____

   _____

Copying is illegal. Measuring Up® to the New York Common Core

On Your Own

Read the story and identify its important events and details.

Avalanche!

Science
Connection

Natasha and her parents were staying in a cabin at the foot of Mount Ember. It was early spring, and the mountain was still snow-covered. Every day the family skied or put on snowshoes and hiked in the powdery snow.

One afternoon, Natasha was making a snack in the kitchen when she heard a strange, low rumbling noise. "Mom, what is that?" she called out.

"I don't know," her mother said, coming into the kitchen and looking out the window. Then she gasped and cried, "Look at the mountain! It's an avalanche!"

Natasha could see a huge wave of snow pouring down the mountain as if it were water. The cabin seemed to be right in its path. She screamed, and she and her mother ran to the door, but her father stopped them.

"It's all right," he said calmly. "The cabin owner told us this happens sometimes. It looks like it's headed right here, but it will pass us by—the avalanche path is way to the side."

Sure enough, as the family watched, amazed and anxious, the giant wall of snow rushed past the cabin and down the mountain, as loud as a train. A moment later, it was as if nothing had ever happened.

Complete the activities based on the passage you just read.

1 Who is this selection about?

_____

_____

2 What detail do you need to know about where the characters are?

_____

_____

3 In your own words, tell what Natasha hears.

_____

_____

4 What does Natasha see out the window?

A an avalanche

B a skier

C her father

D a mountain

5 Which of these details do you need to know?

A The family hikes on snowshoes.

B The mountain is snow-covered.

C Natasha screams.

D Natasha is making a snack.

6 What detail about Natasha's father do you need to know?

_____

_____

7 What do you need to know about the wall of snow?

_____

_____

Elevate **8** On your own sheet of paper, write a summary of the story. Include important events and details and use your own words. Next, compare your summary with the summaries two partners wrote. Which information did all three of you include? Which information did only one or two of you include? Discuss why. Then, work together to write a summary all three of you agree on.

Copying is illegal. Measuring Up® to the New York Common Core

Explore how stories are retold and practice summarizing stories by competing the following activity.

Critical Thinking

9 Summaries and retellings of older stories have much in common. Both keep only the most important parts. Work with a partner. Find a children's book that is a retelling of another story. Then find a copy of the original story and compare them. Select two related portions of text and decide how the rewriter's skill turned one into the other. Finally, create a display that shows the portions of text side by side. Take turns explaining what you think was the rewriter's thought process as he or she created the retelling. Save a recording of the session for the class library.

Lesson 15

Understanding Character

RL.4.3	Describe in depth a character, setting, or event in a story or drama, drawing on specific details in the text.
RL.4.11	Recognize, interpret, and make connections in narratives, poetry, and drama to other texts, ideas, cultural perspectives, personal events, and situations. **a.** Self-select text based upon personal preferences.
CCR.R.3	Analyze how and why individuals, events, and ideas develop and interact over the course of a text.

 ## Understand the Standards

Imagine you are reading a story for class about a girl who is trying to solve a mystery. You come to this passage:

> Amanda had always been afraid of the dark. She looked for a light at the top of the cellar stairs, but there wasn't a switch. She took a deep breath, squared her shoulders, and started slowly down the stairs.

The story is about Amanda. You learn a lot about her from this passage. The writer tells you that she has always been afraid of the dark. You also find out that even though she is afraid, she will go down the stairs. This tells you that Amanda is brave.

Amanda is a character in the story. A **character** is someone in a story, poem, or play. The **main character** is the most important character.

Characters have **traits**, or personal qualities. You can learn about a character's traits by noticing the following:

- what the writer says directly about the character

- what the character says and does

- the character's cultural background

- the character's relationships with other characters

Characters have motivations for what they do and say. A character's **motivation** is the reason why he or she acts. To figure out a character's motivation for acting, notice how the character feels or what he or she wants.

Words to Know
character
main character
traits
motivation

Guided Instruction

When you read a story, pay close attention to the characters, especially the main character. Think about the character's traits and motivation.

Vote for Tim!

Tim stood at the podium and looked out over the classroom, as he finished his speech. "I want to be your class president," he said. "But I need your help to get there, and if I get there, I need your help to succeed."

The class clapped, but then Janis spoke up and said, "You're new here, and we don't know you very well. What makes you think you'd be the best president?"

"I don't know if I'd be the best," Tim said shyly. "But I want to do what's best for the class, and I have a lot of ideas. Are you with me?"

There was a moment of silence, and then Janis said, "Yes, I am!" The rest of the class erupted into cheers.

Guided Questions

Who is the main character? How do you know?

_____

_____

_____

_____

How do you learn more about the main character—from what the writer tells you about him or her or from what the main character tells you about him- or herself?

_____

_____

_____

_____

_____

Would you vote for Tim based on what he said in his speech?

_____

_____

_____

_____

Complete the following activity based on the passage you just read.

1. Fill in the chart with information about Tim.

What the writer tells you	What Tim's words and actions tell you	What other characters tell you

On Your Own

Real World Connection

Read the story. Think about the characters, their traits, and their motivations. Then answer the questions.

Cleanup Crew

Carlos stood and looked over the lake. From a distance, it was still beautiful, but up close he could see the garbage, the discarded tires, and other junk along the shore. He sighed deeply and then turned to his friends.

"All right, guys," he said with determination. "It's going to be a tough job, but I think we can clean this place up."

"It's so much work," Michael complained. "Why should we do it?"

Carlos got angry, and his eyes flashed. "Because Lake Waneta was once beautiful, and it can be again, because we're strong enough to do the work, and because once it's clean again, we'll have a place to swim and fish. Are you in or not?"

Michael smiled. "I guess I'd better be in, right? When you get like this, I've got no choice, so lead on!"

Carlos turned to the other boys and said, "Let's make a line, and we can pass the trash down it—that way we'll get through the big stuff quickly." The boys set to work, and by sundown, the shoreline was perfectly clean.

Answer the questions based on the passage.

1 Who is the main character?

_____

2 What does the writer tell you about Carlos?

_____

3 What does Carlos's anger tell you about him?

_____

_____

_____

4 One word that describes Carlos is

A *cheerful.*

B *uncertain.*

C *cautious.*

D *forceful.*

5 What is Carlos's motivation for cleaning up the lake?

_____

_____

_____

6 What do you learn about Carlos from his relationship with Michael?

_____

_____

_____

 7 On your own sheet of paper, write a brief character sketch of Carlos. Include details about what the writer tells you, what Carlos says and does, and Carlos's relationships with others. Then work with a group of classmates to identify a problem area like Lake Waneta in your own community. Explain why it is a problem and how you and your fellow students could make it better.

Critical Thinking

8 List characteristics of the kinds of things you like to read and what you don't. Refine this list over the school year. Ask your teachers and local librarians to help you find more books that are similar to the things you like. Set a reading goal for yourself for the rest of the school year. Can you read a book a week? Can you read even more?

_____

_____

_____

_____

_____

 Measuring Up® to the New York Common Core

Understanding Setting

RL.4.3	Describe in depth a character, setting, or event in a story or drama, drawing on specific details in the text.
CCR.R.3	Analyze how and why individuals, events, and ideas develop and interact over the course of a text.
CCR.SL.1	Prepare for and participate effectively in a range of conversations and collaborations with diverse partners, building on others' ideas and expressing their own clearly and persuasively.

 ## Understand the Standards

When you read a story or see a movie or television show, the **setting**, or time and place it occurs, can tell you a lot. Imagine you come across this description in a story you are reading for class:

> **Words to Know**
> setting

> Huge tree-like plants reached for the purple sky, and the light from three moons made it almost as bright as day would be on Earth. Underfoot, mossy plants cushioned Hector's steps. He longed to remove his helmet to see if he could breathe in the air of this strange, beautiful place.

Details in the story tell you when and where it takes place. The plants are strange, there are three moons in the sky, and the main character doesn't know if he can breathe the air. You can tell that the story takes place on another planet, probably in the future.

To figure out the setting of a story, follow these steps:

- Use details in the text and illustrations to identify where the story takes place.

- Use details in the text and illustrations to identify when the story takes place.

- Create a mental picture of the time and place, using the details.

- Notice if the time and place change as the story goes on.

The setting of a story can affect the characters and the events. Knowing when and where a story takes place can help you understand why characters act in a certain way and why certain events happen.

Guided Instruction

When you read a story, notice the details that tell you about the setting. Think about how the setting might affect the characters and events.

City Winter

"I don't know how people can live in this city," Will complained, pacing around the little apartment. "There's no *nature*—how can you even tell what season it is?"

Sachiko laughed and replied, "You're such a country boy! We have nature, but you have to look a little harder for it." She led Will to the apartment window, and they looked out at the night. In the glow of the streetlights, snow had started to fall gently, blanketing the streets and skyscrapers with a dusting of white.

"Oh!" Will said in wonderment. "It makes everything look so different, and so beautiful!"

Guided Questions
What do Will and his friend Sachiko disagree about?
How is the conflict between them resolved?
How does the illustration help you understand the importance of the setting?

Answer and discuss these questions about the passage.

1. Where is this story set?

_____

2. What details tell you about the setting?

_____

_____

3. How does the setting affect Will?

_____

 Measuring Up® to the New York Common Core

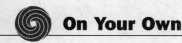

On Your Own

Read the story. Think about the setting and how it affects the characters and events. Then answer the questions.

 **The Crossing**

Ellie woke when the covered wagon came to a halt. She scrambled to the front of the wagon and looked out. In the dawn light, she could see a broad river just ahead.

"Climb out, Ellie," her father instructed. "We have to try to ford the river."

There was no way to tell how deep the water was, so Ellie's father walked ahead of the team, leading them. The water rose to his waist, then his chest, and Ellie watched fearfully as the horses scrabbled for a foothold on the rocky bottom. The tall wheels of the wagon were submerged, and the horses were looking panicky. If the water got any deeper, they would have to swim. They reached the middle of the river, and then, as her father walked on, the water gradually grew shallower and the horses calmed. They scrambled up to the opposite bank, and Ellie realized she would have to swim across to join them. She stepped in, wincing at the icy feel of the water that had tumbled down from the snow-covered peaks they had just crossed. It rose to her waist, and then her feet left the bottom and she paddled desperately, her long skirts pulling her down. Just when she thought she could go no farther, she felt her father's strong hand on her arm, and she stood, dripping and shivering, as the sun's warm light spread across the river.

Answer the questions based on the passage.

1 Where does the story take place?

_____

_____

2 When does the story take place?

_____

_____

3 What details tell you when the story takes place?

_____

_____

4 When the events happen, it is

   A midnight.

   B dawn.

   C midday.

   D evening.

5 The river water is cold because

   A it comes from mountain snow.

   B it is wintertime.

   C it is nighttime.

   D the ice has just melted.

6 How does the place where the story occurs affect the characters?

_____

_____

7 How does the time when the story occurs affect the events of the story?

_____

_____

_____

Elevate **8** Brainstorm with a group of students how you could rewrite the story, setting it in the present or in the future. Decide on conflicts or problems that could arise in each setting and how some change in the setting, like the snow falling in "City Winter," could resolve the conflict. Then, on your own sheet of paper, rewrite the story. Include details that tell about the new setting. Add an illustration that shows something important about the setting.

Understanding Plot and Plot Patterns

RL.4.3	Describe in depth a character, setting, or event in a story or drama, drawing on specific details in the text.
RL.4.9	Compare and contrast the treatment of similar themes and topics and patterns of events in stories, myths, and traditional literature from different cultures.
CCR.R.3	Analyze how and why individuals, events, and ideas develop and interact over the course of a text.

⟲ Understand the Standards

When you tell your teacher or your class what happens in a story, you are telling the story's **plot**. The plot is the series of events that happen. Usually, the plot involves a problem that the main character must solve. The character faces a **conflict**, or struggle.

Words to Know

plot
conflict
climax
resolution

Multicultural Connection

> Jason's task was to find the Golden Fleece and return home with it. The Fleece, however, was guarded by a sleepless dragon.

This part of the story tells you that Jason's problem is getting the Golden Fleece from a sleepless dragon. The conflict in the story is between Jason and the dragon.

To identify the plot of a story, notice these elements:

- the beginning or introduction, which tells about the characters and setting and introduces the problem or conflict

- the events that tell how the main character tries to solve the problem

- the **climax**, or most exciting moment

- the events that lead to the end

- the **resolution**, when the problem is solved or the conflict is resolved

Sometimes stories from different times or different cultures will have similar plots. Notice how the events are the same and how they are different.

Guided Instruction

When you read a story, notice the events that take place. Think about the problem or conflict and what the main character does to solve it.

Literature Connection

The Second Labor of Hercules

The second of Hercules' 12 impossible tasks was to kill the Hydra, a poisonous water beast with seven heads. If any of her heads were cut off, she grew two more.

Bravely, Hercules dove into the lake where the Hydra lived, covering his mouth with a cloth to keep from tasting the poison. At the entrance to the Underworld he found the Hydra. With his sword he cut off each head, dipping the sword in the Hydra's poison and rubbing it on each neck so no new heads would grow. One of the Hydra's heads was immortal, though. This head he placed under a rock, and there it lies still.

Guided Questions

What words in the first paragraph tell you that Hercules can do heroic things?

_____

_____

_____

What is the setting? How does the setting make the conflict with the Hydra sound even more frightening?

_____

_____

_____

_____

_____

_____

What character traits help Hercules overcome the Hydra?

_____

_____

What event does the last sentence of the story suggest could happen?

_____

_____

_____

 Measuring Up® to the New York Common Core

Fill in this story map.

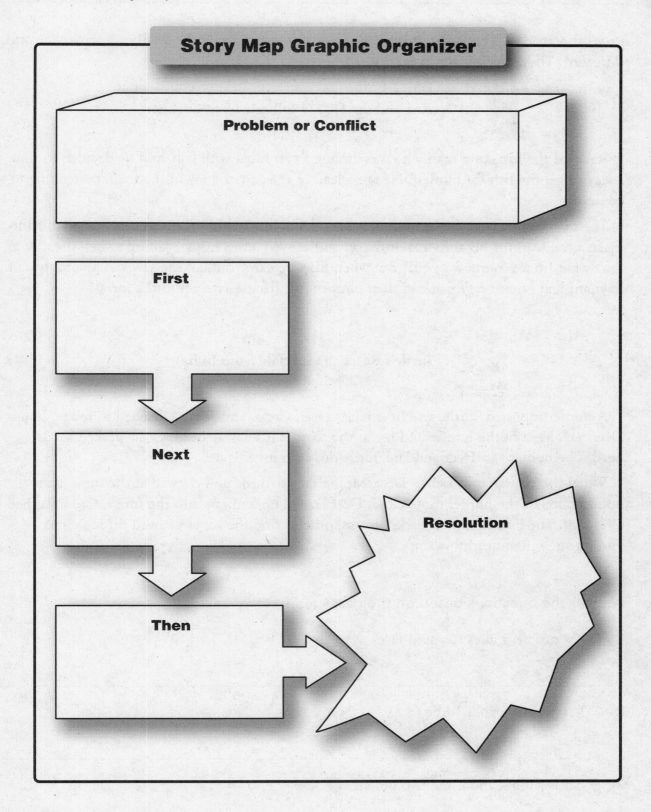

Story Map Graphic Organizer

Problem or Conflict

First

Next

Then

Resolution

On Your Own

Read the stories. Think about what happens in the plots and how they are similar and different. Then answer the questions.

 Literature Connection

Reynard and the Fish (a folktale from Europe)

Reynard the fox saw a man who was driving a cart filled with fish, and he decided to find a way to get the fish for himself. He ran ahead of the cart and lay in the road, pretending to be dead.

The man came upon the fox and, thinking it was dead, threw it in his cart. He planned to make a fox scarf for his wife. He drove on and arrived at his home, calling to his wife, "Wife, look what I have found for you!" But when his wife came out, all she saw was an empty cart. Reynard had eaten every fish and then jumped off, fleeing safely into the forest.

 Multicultural Connection

Turtle's Rescue (a folktale from India)

A hunter captured Turtle, and his friends Deer, Crow, and Mouse decided to rescue him. Deer ran ahead of the hunter and lay in the road as if he were dead. Crow pecked at his head. The hunter saw Deer and laid Turtle down to investigate.

When the hunter approached Deer, Mouse ran to Turtle and chewed at the ropes that bound him. As the hunter came close, Deer leaped up and ran into the forest. Crow flapped after him. The hunter turned back, furious, only to find the ropes gnawed through and Turtle gone into a nearby swamp.

Answer the questions based on the passage.

1 What problem does Reynard face?

_____

2 What problem does Turtle face?

_____

3 What is similar about the two plots?

_____

4 The first event in "Reynard and the Fish" is

  A Reynard runs ahead of the cart.

  B the man picks up Reynard.

  C Reynard sees a cart full of fish.

  D Reynard eats the fish.

5 The climax of "Turtle's Rescue" comes when

  A Deer and Crow run away.

  B Deer pretends to be dead.

  C Mouse chews on the ropes.

  D Turtle is captured.

6 How does Reynard solve his problem?

  _____

  _____

  _____

7 How is Turtle's problem solved?

  _____

  _____

  _____

 8 On your own sheet of paper, explain what event occurs in both stories and tell how the event leads to each story's resolution. Then work with a partner to make a Story Map Graphic Organizer for each On Your Own story. Agree on what should appear in each part of the organizer.

Comparing and Contrasting Point of View

RL.4.6	Compare and contrast the point of view from which different stories are narrated, including the difference between first- and third-person narrations.
CCR.R.6	Assess how point of view or purpose shapes the content and style of a text.
CCR.SL.1	Prepare for and participate effectively in a range of conversations and collaborations with diverse partners, building on others' ideas and expressing their own clearly and persuasively.

Understand the Standards

When you read a story for class, you might talk about who tells the story. The person who tells a story is the **narrator**. Sometimes the narrator is a person in the story. In other stories, the narrator is a person outside the story who is telling what happens.

Words to Know

narrator
first-person point of view
third-person point of view

- Some stories are told in the **first-person point of view**. In these stories, the narrator is part of the story. The narrator uses the words *I*, *me*, and *my* to tell the story from his or her point of view. In a story told in the first-person point of view, you can only know what the narrator wants you to know.

  I ran as fast as I could, but the other racers were gaining on me. I could hear them panting as they came closer and closer.

- Some stories use **third-person point of view**. In these stories, the narrator is not a character in the story. The narrator can focus on a single character or can tell what many characters are seeing and feeling. In these stories, the narrator uses the words *he*, *she*, *him*, and *her* to refer to characters.

  Manuel ran as fast as he could, but the other racers were gaining on him. Teddy came closer and closer, panting and pushing himself to go faster.

Measuring Up® to the New York Common Core

Guided Instruction

When you read a story, think about the point of view. Consider who the narrator is and what you can learn about the characters.

Snow Joy

Sports Connection

"Are you sure this is safe—what if I can't stop?" I asked Mr. Uchida, the snowboard instructor.

Mr. Uchida laughed. "We've practiced stopping over and over, and I know you're ready, Matilda. I'll be right next to you, so don't worry—I really think you'll enjoy it."

I took a deep breath, pointed my snowboard down the slope, and in an instant was zipping downhill, faster than I would have thought possible. The wind whistled past me, and I forgot my fear as I felt the joy of speed. I saw Mr. Uchida's delighted face as he sped down beside me, and we stopped easily at the bottom of the hill, laughing and whooping.

Guided Questions
As you read the story, when do you find out who the narrator is? Why?
_____
_____
_____
Why is the narrator not certain before then?
_____
_____
_____
_____
_____
_____
_____

Answer and discuss these questions about the passage.

1. From what point of view is this story told?

_____

2. How can you determine the story's point of view?

_____

3. What would the narrator of this story not know about Mr. Uchida?

_____

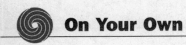 **On Your Own**

Read the story. Think about point of view. Then answer the questions.

Surprise!

Peter walked into the house, which was strangely quiet. "Hello," he called uncertainly, "is anybody home?" There was no answer, and he wandered from the hallway into the study, then into the living room. The whole place was deserted, so he looked around for a note telling him where his parents had gone, what his sister was doing. Funny, but none of his friends was around either—Jonas wasn't biking down the street as he usually was, and Robin wasn't working in her father's store when he'd stopped by on his way home.

"I'll just get a snack," Peter told himself uneasily, heading for the kitchen. The swinging door was closed, which was also odd, and he began to feel a little afraid. What was going on?

He pushed the door open and felt for the light switch. Suddenly, the light went on by itself, and a chorus of voices shouted, "Surprise!" There, crowded into the kitchen, were Peter's parents, his sister, Jonas and Robin, and half a dozen other friends from school. On the kitchen table was a big, beautiful chocolate cake, blazing with candles.

"But . . . but my birthday isn't until tomorrow!" Peter protested, stunned, and Robin laughed.

"If we'd done this tomorrow, you might have expected it," she pointed out, pleased with the success of the surprise. Peter, grinning at last, had to admit that she was right.

Answer the questions based on the passage.

1 From what point of view is the story told?

_____

2 How can you determine the point of view?

_____

_____

3 In the first paragraph, how does the narrator let you know how Peter feels?

_____

_____

4 The narrator lets you know that Peter is surprised by using the word

A uneasily.

B crowded.

C stunned.

D grinning.

5 How would you best describe the narrator of the story?

A a friend of Peter

B a person outside the story

C a character in the story

D the story's main character

6 How would this sentence be written in the first-person point of view?

He pushed the door open and felt for the light switch.

_____

7 What does this narrator know that a first-person narrator would not know?

_____

 8 On your own sheet of paper, rewrite the first paragraph of the story "Surprise!" using a first-person point of view. Remember to include only the information and details the narrator would know. Then work with a partner to rewrite "Snow Joy" from Mr. Uchida's point of view. Decide which paragraphs you do not have to change. Finally, list the problems you solved when you rewrote each story. Which one was the harder to rewrite? Why?

RL.4.2	Determine the theme of a story, drama, or poem.
RL.4.9	Compare and contrast the treatment of similar themes and topics in stories, myths, and traditional literature from different cultures.
CCR.R.2	Determine central ideas or themes of a text and analyze their development.
CCR.R.9	Analyze how two or more texts address similar themes.
CCR.R.11	Respond to literature by employing knowledge of literary language, textual features, and forms to read and comprehend, reflect upon, and interpret literary texts from a variety of genres and a wide spectrum of American and world cultures.
CCR.SL.1	Prepare for and participate effectively in a range of conversations and collaborations with diverse partners.

 ## Understand the Standards

Have you ever read a story and realized it has taught you something about life? The message or lesson about life that a story provides is called the **theme.**

> **Words to Know**
> theme
> universal

Some themes are **universal.** You can find them in stories written in different places and at different times. Often, a theme can be expressed as a short statement about life or people in general, such as the following:

Friendship is worth more than money.

Hard work can be its own reward.

Change can be positive.

When you want to identify the theme of a story, follow these steps:

- Think about what the characters do and say. How do they change? What do they learn?

- Consider the conflict or problem the main character faces. What does he or she have to do?

- Think about your own experiences. How would you act in the main character's place? Have you ever had a similar experience? If so, what did you learn?

- Decide what the writer is trying to say about life or people in general.

Guided Instruction

When you read a story, think about the message, or theme. Consider what the characters do, say, and learn in the story.

All Together Now

It was the last inning of the baseball game, and Ty's team was losing by three runs. "We're never going to win," Allan said, discouraged, "so we might as well not even try."

"We're a team," Ty insisted, "and we're as good as they are. Give it your best, and at least we can say we tried."

Allan nodded, went up to bat, and hit a line drive, running to first base. Then the next batter hit a single, and the next one hit another single, and now there were three players on base. Ty walked up to home plate, and as he looked at his teammates on first, second, and third base, each one gave him a thumbs-up. The pitch came in, and Ty swung hard—it was a home run! He sprinted around the bases, and his team ran to him as he came home. "You were right," Allan said. "We did it—we won the game!"

Guided Questions

Can you tell in a few words what the story is about?

_____

_____

_____

_____

_____

_____

_____

What conflict did Allan and Ty face?

_____

_____

_____

_____

Do you agree with the message about life that the story presents? Why?

_____

_____

_____

_____

_____

Answer and discuss these questions about the passage.

1. What words of Ty's affected Allan?

_____

2. How did Allan change in the story?

_____

3. What is the theme of the story?

_____

 On Your Own

Read the stories. Talk with a partner about the themes.

 The Woodman and the Axe

Multicultural
Connection

A woodman was cutting trees by the river, and after one mighty swipe, the axe jumped from his hands and fell in the water, sinking into its depths. As he stood sadly gazing into the river, the god Mercury appeared and asked him what was wrong. "I have lost my axe and cannot make a living," the woodman told him.

Mercury dove into the river and came up with a golden axe. "Is this yours?" he asked the woodman. The woodman looked longingly at the golden axe, but he shook his head. Mercury dove again, bringing up the woodman's axe. "Is this yours?" he asked, and the woodman nodded and thanked him graciously. Pleased with the woodman's honesty, Mercury gave him the golden axe as a gift.

 The Runaway Tennis Ball

Sports
Connection

James hit the tennis ball against the wall over and over, practicing his swing. On one hit, though, he swung too hard. The ball flew over the wall, and James heard a crash that made his heart sink. A moment later, Mr. Santos appeared, holding the tennis ball.

"Is this yours?" he asked James, and James looked at the other tennis players on the courts nearby, tempted to blame them. Then he hung his head and admitted that the ball was his.

"Well, you can help me repair my window, and you can work in my garden to earn the money to pay for the repair," Mr. Sanchez said. "And then, if you want, you can keep working for me, and I'll pay you. I need a boy who can tell the truth!"

Complete the following activities based on the passages you just read.

1 What problem does the woodman face?

_____

2 What problem does James face?

_____

3 What do both main characters learn?

_____

4 The main conflict the characters in both stories face is between

A staying and running away.

B lying and telling the truth.

C fighting and giving up.

D helping another and helping themselves.

5 Mr. Sanchez's words show that he

A is angry at James.

B wants revenge.

C values honesty.

D does not like James.

6 What effect do the actions of the woodman and James have?

_____

7 What theme do both stories share?

_____

Critical Thinking

8 On your own sheet of paper, explain whether you think the theme is true for people in general. Then discuss the stories with a partner. Decide which of the stories affected you most as a person, the story from Greek mythology or the modern-day story. Explain why. Then discuss why people today continue to read stories from Greek mythology. Why do stories like "The Woodman and the Axe" still mean something to people after thousands of years?

Lesson 20

Connecting Versions of a Story

RL.4.7	Make connections between the text of a story or drama and a visual or oral presentation of the text, identifying where each version reflects specific descriptions and directions in the text.
CCR.R.7	Integrate and evaluate content presented in diverse media and formats, including visually and quantitatively, as well as in words.
CCR.SL.1	Prepare for and participate effectively in a range of conversations and collaborations with diverse partners, building on others' ideas and expressing their own clearly and persuasively.

Understand the Standards

Media Connection

Many stories or poems you read are popular enough to be presented in other versions. These versions include:

> **Words to Know**
> recordings

- Plays. Many well-known stories have been made into plays to be presented on the stage.

- Movies. Stories and even some poems have been made into movies to be watched on a screen.

- Comic books. Some well-known stories have been redone in comic book or graphic novel form.

- **Recordings**. Many stories and poems have been read aloud and recorded on audio discs.

When you read, see, or hear a familiar story or poem in a different form, you will notice some changes. A movie version of a story may be more dramatic or may leave out part of the plot. A play version will include stage directions and will show the action through dialogue and characters' movements on the stage. A comic book version of a story will probably show only some of the action and may include dialogue in speech balloons. Different versions of a work will have connections, too. They will usually feature the same characters. The plot will be basically the same.

Guided Instruction

When you look at different versions of a work, think about how they are connected.

from **Alice in Wonderland**
by Lewis Carroll

The Cat only grinned when it saw Alice. It looked good-natured, she thought: still it had *very* long claws and a great many teeth, so she felt that it ought to be treated with respect.

"Cheshire-Puss," she began, rather timidly, as she did not at all know whether it would like the name: however, it only grinned a little wider. "Come, it's pleased so far," thought Alice, and she went on: "Would you tell me, please, which way I ought to go from here?"

Guided Questions

Why do books often include illustrations like this one?

_____

_____

_____

What did the illustrator leave out from the text version of the scene? Why?

_____

_____

_____

_____

_____

_____

_____

What is the expression on Alice's face in the illustration trying to express? Is it successful?

_____

_____

Answer and discuss these questions about the passage and the illustration.

1. How are the description of the Cheshire Cat and the cat in the illustration similar?

_____

2. How are the description and the illustration different?

_____

_____

 On Your Own

Read the poem and the play aloud with a partner. Talk with your partner about how they are connected. Then answer the questions.

Sports
Connection

from **Casey at the Bat**
by Ernest Thayer

Ten thousand eyes were on him as he rubbed his hands with dirt;
Five thousand tongues applauded when he wiped them on his shirt.
Then while the writhing pitcher ground the ball into his hip,
Defiance gleamed in Casey's eye, a sneer curled Casey's lip.

And now the leather-covered sphere came hurtling through the air,
And Casey stood a-watching it in haughty grandeur there.
Close by the sturdy batsman the ball unheeded sped-
"That ain't my style," said Casey. "Strike one," the umpire said.

From the benches, black with people, there went up a muffled roar,
Like the beating of the storm-waves on a stern and distant shore.
"Kill him! Kill the umpire!" shouted someone on the stand;
And it's likely they'd a-killed him had not Casey raised his hand.

Music/Arts
Connection

from **No Joy in Mudville**

(Casey stands at the plate, sneering. The pitcher throws the ball.)

CASEY: *(without moving)* That ain't my style.

UMPIRE: Strike one! *(The crowd roars.)*

PERSON IN STANDS: Kill him! Kill the umpire! *(The crowd rushes forward.)*

(Casey raises his hand.)

Answer the questions based on the passages.

1 How does the play show the action that takes place?

_____

2 What is the greatest similarity between the two works?

_____

3 In the poem, the ball goes by "unheeded." In the play, which stage directions show this?

   A *sneering*

   B *throws the ball*

   C *holds up his hand*

   D *without moving*

4 In both versions, Casey

   A holds up his hand.

   B sneers.

   C swings.

   D shouts, "Kill the umpire!"

5 The stage directions in the play state *The crowd rushes forward*. What line from the poem does this reflect?

_____

6 The poem clearly tells how the crowd feels. How could you know how they feel if you were watching the play?

_____

 7 The poem includes details that are not in the play version. Discuss with a partner to decide and list how the versions are different. Then write a summary of what you decided. Explain what information in the poem would have to be shown by actors onstage in the play version.

Story Vocabulary: Allusions to Literature

RL.4.4	Determine the meaning of words and phrases as they are used in a text, including those that allude to significant characters found in mythology.
RL.4.10	By the end of the year, read and comprehend literature, including stories, dramas, and poetry, in the grades 4–5 text complexity band proficiently, with scaffolding as needed at the high end of the range.
CCR.R.4	Interpret words and phrases as they are used in a text, including determining technical, connotative, and figurative meanings, and analyze how specific word choices shape meaning or tone.
CCR.SL.1	Prepare for and participate effectively in a range of conversations and collaborations with diverse partners, building on others' ideas and expressing their own clearly and persuasively.

 ## Understand the Standards

Sometimes when you read, you will come across a reference to another story you know. Here is an example:

> **Words to Know**
> allusion

The room was as long and high as the dining room in Hogwarts.

If you know the Harry Potter stories, you can imagine just what the room looks like—huge, with tall windows and long tables.

A reference to a person, place, or thing in literature or history is called an **allusion**. Writers make allusions to give readers a mental picture or create a mood without having to write a description.

Many allusions refer to characters or events from mythology.

With a Herculean effort, Henry held up the table as I jammed its leg back in place.

Multicultural Connection The word *Herculean* refers to the Greek character Hercules, who was known for his incredible strength. By alluding to Hercules, the writer creates a mental picture of Henry's great effort in holding up the table.

Measuring Up® to the New York Common Core

Guided Instruction

When you come across words in a story that allude to other works, think about why the writer used them.

The Odyssey, written in ancient Greece by the poet Homer, tells of Odysseus's 10-year journey by ship back from Troy to his home island of Ithaca. It describes his many adventures and the dangers he faced. Keep the tale in mind as you read this passage.

The Long Way Home

We waited anxiously for Dad to get home after his first day at the new job. Dinner grew cold on the table, and I could see that Mom was really beginning to worry when at last the door opened and my tired father came in.

"I'm sorry I'm late," he told us, "but my trip home was a real odyssey. The 5:45 train was canceled, and then the next train stopped in the tunnel with some kind of electrical failure. We had to get off the train and walk through the tunnel in the dark, then wait for still another train. That one was too full, so we had to keep waiting, and then, when we were finally home, there was a cow on the tracks! So we had to wait until they moved it." We started to laugh, and Dad finally joined in. "The new job was great, though!" he told us, laughing so hard he could barely speak.

Guided Questions

What does the illustration probably depict?

_____

_____

_____

_____

_____

What in the illustration represents the father? What represents the difficulties he faced that day?

_____

_____

_____

_____

_____

Why do you think the father described his trip as an "odyssey"?

_____

_____

_____

_____

_____

Answer and discuss these questions about the passage.

1. What allusion does the writer make?

   _____

2. To what does the allusion refer?

   _____

3. What effect does the allusion have?

   _____

   _____

On Your Own

Read the passage. Talk with a partner about the underlined allusions. Then answer the questions.

Soccer Showdown

Sports Connection

Our team stood facing the team from P.S. 142, and we trembled. "Those girls are <u>gigantic</u>!" Maria whispered to me.

I nodded and replied, "They're real <u>Amazons</u>—we're going to have to outrun them."

We kept up with the girls from P.S. 142 for three quarters, as they barreled their way up and down the field. We were small, but we were fast, and we managed to score two goals while they tripped over their own feet trying to find us. It was easy enough to steal the ball from them. We danced around them, laughing as they grew furious with our speed and <u>grace</u>.

The last quarter was <u>chaos</u>, though, as we grew tired from all that running and the other team managed to knock in two goals themselves. "We're really going to need some good <u>fortune</u> if we're going to win this game," Maria said, panting with exhaustion. With a <u>titanic</u> effort, we kept them from scoring again as the minutes counted down.

"I feel like I've run ten miles," I told Maria, "but we have to keep going. It's time for our <u>swan song</u>!" Maria snared the ball and began to race downfield with it. In moments, despite her tiredness, she had placed herself directly in front of the goal, and she let go with a beautiful kick just as the referee blew the whistle. Goal!

Answer the questions based on the passage.

1 In Greek mythology, the Giants or Gigantes were the enormous children of the goddess Gaia. When Maria calls the other team "gigantic," to what physical trait does the allusion refer?

_____

2 What image does the allusion create?

_____

3 In Greek mythology, the Amazons were women who were known for being great warriors. When the narrator calls the other team "Amazons," what image does the allusion create?

_____

4 In mythology, chaos was the state of the universe before anything existed. What does the narrator describe as "chaos"?

A the last quarter of the game

B her team

C the other team

D the last goal

5 The writer uses the word *chaos* to suggest

A a lot of noise.

B absolute darkness.

C a condition of confusion.

D a condition of fear.

6 The Furies were goddesses of revenge in mythology who punished those who made false promises. When the narrator describes the other team as "furious," what does she mean?

_____

7 The Graces were Roman goddesses of beauty, charm, and creativity. When the narrator claims her teammates moved with "grace," what does she mean?

_____

8 The story includes the words *titanic* and *fortune* and the phrase *swan song*, which all allude to mythology. Work with three partners. Each of you will choose one of the words or the phrase, look up its origins, and write a paragraph explaining what it means and its effect on the passage. Revise your paragraphs together until you agree on the conclusions. Finally, combine your paragraphs into a report that you present to the class.

Critical Thinking

9 The names of the planets in the solar system are allusions to Greek and Roman gods. Work with a partner to make a chart. On it, list all eight planets plus the dwarf planet Pluto. Next to each, tell some interesting facts about the name of the planet. Include some of their moons, too, if their names are interesting. Include photographs and add a diagram showing their positions. Share your chart with classmates.

Dramatize a Story

Media Connection

Work with a group to choose a scene from a story that you would like to make into a play. Talk with your group about how the play version should connect to the original story and how it should be different. Then follow these steps.

- Choose a director to be in charge.

- Decide who will play each character in the play.

- Write the dialogue for each character.

- Work together to rehearse the scene. If possible, find props and costumes that will work in the scene.

- Perform the scene for your class or a larger group. If you can, have a friend make a video of your performance.

Locate a Setting

Geography Connection

With a partner, think of a story that is set in another state or another country. Look closely at the setting details of the story. Using a paint software program, work with your partner to draw an illustration of the setting. Alternately, you and your partner can find a photograph of the setting on the Internet and print it out.

When you know exactly what the setting looks like to you, locate it on a map. Print out a blank map of the United States or of the country where the story is set. Find the state, city, or town where the story takes place and label it on the map. Then display your map and illustration or photograph for the class.

Compare Origin Tales

Multicultural Connection

Work with a partner. Using books of folktales or the Internet, find two folktales or myths from different cultures that explain the same aspect of the natural world. Some possibilities include:

- how humans got fire

- how the sun and moon were formed

- how rainbows were formed

- how the stars were placed in the sky

- how the seasons came to be

Copy or print out your stories and practice reading them aloud. Then read them to the class. Discuss with classmates how the stories treat the same theme differently and how they are similar.

Pair Up on Poems

Literature Connection

With a partner, look in books of poetry or on the Internet to find poems about a particular topic, such as the sea, horses, baseball, or another topic of your choice. Choose one poem written from the first-person point of view and another poem written from the third-person point of view. Print out or copy the poems.

You and your partner can each choose one of the poems and practice reading the poems aloud. Give a reading for the class. If possible, make a video of your partner's reading and have your partner video yours. Then discuss the ways in which the points of view made the poems different.

Lesson 22

Identifying Main Idea

RI.4.2	Determine the main idea of a text and explain how it is supported by key details; summarize the text.
RI.4.10	By the end of year, read and comprehend informational texts, including history/social studies, science, and technical texts, in the grades 4–5 text complexity band proficiently, with scaffolding as needed at the high end of the range.
SL.4.3	Identify the reasons and evidence a speaker provides to support particular points.
W.4.2	Write informative/explanatory texts to examine a topic and convey ideas and information clearly. **c.** Link ideas within categories of information using words and phrases.
CCR.R.2	Determine central ideas or themes of a text and analyze their development; summarize the key supporting details and ideas.

Understand the Standards

Identifying the main idea, or **theme**, in a piece of informational writing helps you to understand what you read. Knowing the key idea in what you read will help you to quickly identify what the writing is about. Then you can see how the author uses supporting details to help explain the main idea.

> **Words to Know**
> theme
> topic sentence
> supporting ideas
> summarize

- Often the main idea, or theme, appears as the **topic sentence** in a paragraph.

    Example: Bathing a dog is a challenging process. Follow these steps or you'll spend most of your time cleaning up afterward!

- The author uses **supporting ideas** to explain the main idea in more detail.

    Example: Wear old clothes, be careful if you bathe a big dog in the bathtub, and have plenty of old towels on hand for the dog and you! Start by putting dog shampoo on the dog's head and neck. Make lots of suds and then work your way down the dog's back and legs. After he is rinsed, dry him with a towel and keep him indoors until he's dry. Don't forget to give him a treat!

- Authors may **summarize** the main idea in the concluding sentence (or sentences).

    Example: Washing your dog can be fun—if you organize the job before you start!

Guided Instruction

When you begin to read a piece of informational writing, start by identifying the main idea. Ask yourself how each paragraph adds supporting details to the main idea. Notice how each section or paragraph flows from topic to topic as it discusses the main idea in increasing detail.

Social Studies Connection

Be a Good Citizen!

We have rights but also several responsibilities as U.S. citizens. Every two or four years, American citizens have a chance to participate in a very important event. As citizens we get to help decide who will lead our government at local, state, and national levels. Our democracy depends on people who take the time to be informed and then vote. It is our way to make sure that our representative democracy continues. Citizens may also be asked to serve on a jury, since in the United States people are judged by "a jury of their peers." When someone serves on a jury, he or she takes time off from a job or school in order to take part in this process. As citizens, young people may be asked to serve in the Armed Forces. We are also asked to pay taxes and obey the law. A democracy is like anything else. You have to give as well as take to make it work.

Guided Questions

In the first line, what does the word *several* tell the reader?

_____

_____

_____

Which sentence in this passage is the topic sentence?

_____

_____

What are the two main things the topic sentence tells you the passage will be about?

_____

_____

_____

Answer and discuss these questions about the passage. Hints for thinking about and answering questions are given in parentheses.

1. What part of this passage gives readers the best clue about the main idea?

   (Tip: When you read, pay special attention to the title, introduction, and first paragraph. They may give you hints about the main idea of the passage.)

   _____

   _____

 Measuring Up® to the New York Common Core

2. What are the key supporting details in this passage?

(Hint: To summarize the key details of a passage in your own words, it sometimes helps to say them out loud to a partner.)

_____

_____

_____

3. How would you orally summarize the main idea of this passage in one sentence?

(Hint: Think about what the passage is mainly about.)

_____

_____

 On Your Own

Read the passage, then complete the activities.

 Watch Out for Poison Ivy!

Have you ever heard the old saying "Leaflets three, let it be"? This refers to poison ivy, and whoever said that was telling the truth. Poison ivy can make your life miserable for weeks! Read on. Maybe you can learn from my unfortunate experience.

It doesn't take long to know that you have been in poison ivy. In my case, I touched my dog after he ran off the trail when I was on a hike. Here is my advice.

1. Look at photos of poison ivy at different times of year. Notice the leaf patterns. They also have flowers and berries, so learn to recognize them, too. Some varieties are bushes. Others are vines that often wind their way up trees.

2. If you know you've been in it, rinse off in COLD water from a hose. (Hot water opens your pores and makes the poison oil from the plant that most people are allergic to seep into your skin.) Itchy spots can turn into red sores. They can spread everywhere on your body in no time.

3. Get medicine or call your doctor immediately!

4. Make sure you wash your clothes twice, or, in my opinion, take no chances. Throw them away.

Poison ivy (and its cousin, poison oak) grow nearly everywhere in the United States. You can get the oil on your skin by

- touching the plant.
- touching clothing (including shoes), pets, or tools that have touched the plant.
- burning a poison ivy plant and breathing in the smoke.

After all this, I hope you will heed my warning and remember the old saying:

"Leaflets three, let it be!"

Answer the questions based on the passage.

1 Why do you think the rashes can spread so easily on your body?

_____

_____

_____

_____

Discuss

2 After reading this passage, what, in your opinion, would be the worst way to get poison ivy, and why? Take part in a class debate on this issue, making sure you have adequate supporting details to back up your opinion.

_____

_____

_____

_____

3 How does the format call attention to the main idea in the passage?

A The author summarizes the main points at the end.

B The author numbers the main ideas.

C The author makes new paragraphs.

D The author outlines the main ideas in the introduction.

Measuring Up® to the New York Common Core

4 Reread the sentence below.

I touched my dog after he ran off the trail when I was on a hike.

Which sentence most logically follows that sentence?

A Dogs should not be off a leash at any time, especially in forested areas.

B It's easy for dogs to brush up against the plant and get it on their fur.

C My dog Herald never got in poison ivy because he always stayed on the path.

D My dog Rufus is an active dog and a real character, but he's my best friend.

5 What details could you add to point 3 to make it more useful to readers?

_____

_____

_____

6 After reading this passage and using your own imagination, what are some ways an author can organize the main points and details in a piece of writing?

_____

_____

_____

 7 You are writing a book about poison ivy. Work with a partner to research and describe the contents for another chapter on the subject that isn't covered in this passage. Then write a paragraph of information that explains the contents of the new chapter. Tell how it links to the ideas in previous chapters.

RI.4.1	Refer to details and examples in a text when explaining what the text says explicitly and when drawing inferences from the text.
RI.4.2	Determine the main idea of a text and explain how it is supported by key details; summarize the text.
SL.4.1	Engage effectively in a range of collaborative discussions with diverse partners on grade 4 topics and texts, building on others' ideas and expressing their own clearly. **c.** Pose and respond to specific questions to clarify or follow up on information, and make comments that contribute to the discussion and link to the remarks of others.
W.4.2	Write informative/explanatory texts to examine a topic and convey ideas and information clearly. **b.** Develop the topic with facts, definitions, concrete details, quotations, or other information and examples related to the topic.
CCR.R.1	Read closely to determine what the text says explicitly and to make logical inferences; cite specific textual evidence when writing or speaking to support conclusions drawn from the text.
CCR.R.2	Determine central ideas or themes of a text and analyze their development; summarize the key supporting details and ideas.

 ## Understand the Standards

What do private investigators, researchers, and rescue dogs all have in common?

Words to Know
evidence
inferences
explicit

If you said that they all look for **evidence**, or proof, to help them solve a mystery or answer questions, you're right!

When you read for information, you look for clues, too. Sometimes the main idea or the conclusion is clearly stated. Other times, like an investigator, you have to use the evidence presented to reach your own conclusions. Good readers keep track of details as they read. It helps them to answer questions such as:

○ What is the theme or main idea of this text?

○ What evidence in the form of details does the author use to back up what he or she is saying?

○ What logical **inferences**, or conclusions, can be drawn from the evidence presented? (When the inferences are **explicit**, it means that they are stated clearly in the text.)

Guided Instruction

As you read this piece of informational writing about raptors, pay attention to statements of fact made by the author and the evidence given to support each one. What questions do you have as you read? Are your questions answered by the end, or do you need to do further research?

Science Connection

All About Raptors

Have you ever seen a raptor? Raptors are also called birds of prey. There are more than 400 different kinds of raptors all over the world. They live in many different types of habitats, including cities, rugged mountains, coastal regions, and deserts. Some raptors are very small; others, like the Andean condor, weigh more than 30 pounds and have a wingspan of more than 10 feet!

All raptors have several characteristics in common. As birds of prey, these meat-eating birds hunt smaller animals. Some raptors hunt and kill their prey during the day, while others hunt at night.

Raptors have lightweight skeletons with hollow bones braced from the inside. Different wings are designed for specific jobs: Some raptors have huge, strong wings to soar; others have short, thick wings to dart through trees; and still others have slim, pointed wings that are built for speed. Raptors have excellent hearing and sharp eyesight that is about 10 times better than human eyesight. Some, like owls, can see 100 times better than humans in dim light. Three eyelids protect their eyes, including one eyelid that moistens and cleanses their eyes. Their beaks are sharp and curved to pick up and hang on to prey, with the beak size matching the size of the prey. Almost all raptors,

Guided Questions

What is the purpose of each paragraph?

_____

_____

_____

_____

_____

_____

_____

_____

Does the writer use facts or opinions to present information?

_____

_____

except vultures, have long, curved, and very sharp talons, or claws, to help them hunt.

Raptors play a very important part in the ecosystem. They control populations of rodents and tend to hunt weak or sickly animals. Vultures and condors clean up the environment by eating the carcasses of dead animals.

Guided Questions

What do you think the writer's personal opinion about raptors is? Why?

_____

_____

_____

_____

_____

_____

Answer and discuss these questions about the passage. Hints for thinking about and answering questions are given in parentheses.

1. What part of this passage gives readers a first clue about the main idea?

   (Hint: Look for clues in the beginning sections of a piece of writing that tell you what the writing is mainly about.)

   _____

2. What logical inference can you make about raptors' bodies based on information in this passage?

   (Hint: A logical inference is a conclusion based on evidence in the passage.)

   _____

   _____

3. What do you infer from the fact that vultures don't have long, curved, sharp talons like other raptors?

   (Hint: Think about the way vultures get their food and the way other raptors get their food.)

   _____

   _____

On Your Own

Read the passage, then complete the activities.

Science Connection

Turkey Vultures—Fact and Fiction!

Everyone seems to have an opinion about turkey vultures, and rarely is it good. Some people think they're ugly. Many associate them with death, and others think their house pets are in mortal danger of being swooped up by these raptors! Beauty, as they say, is in the eye of the beholder. However, some facts about turkey vultures may help to set the record straight.

Turkey vultures are not aggressive. They do not kill animals, ever. As scavengers, they pick apart and eat the carcasses of already dead animals. They have bodies perfectly designed to do their job as nature's clean-up crew. Since they stick their heads inside the cavities of smelly, dead animals, their bald, featherless heads keep dangerous bacteria and pieces of flesh from sticking to them. They sit in the hot sun after eating and let the sun's heat bake off any remnants of their meal.

Sometimes people think that turkey vultures circle around dead animals, but this is usually not the case. If they spot an animal, they won't wait. They use their keen eyesight and sense of smell to quickly swoop down on their next meal. Turkey vultures have a very advanced sense of smell. Workers trying to locate a leak in their company's gas lines pumped a gas produced by decaying flesh through the lines. Then they waited for turkey vultures to gather where the gas was leaking out.

When turkey vultures circle the sky in graceful arcs, they are simply gliding on pockets of rising warm air. Doesn't that sound fun? Turkey vultures can soar like this for up to six hours without one flap of their huge, broad wings.

The next time you spot a turkey vulture, think about how they make the world a nicer place to live. You might even thank them.

Complete the following activities.

Collaborative Learning

1   Discuss the facts and evidence in this passage with a partner. Then fill in the right-hand column of the chart together.

Turkey Vulture Facts	Evidence in Text
Turkey vultures do not kill animals.	
Their bodies are specially designed to do the job they do.	
Turkey vultures don't circle over dead animals.	
Turkey vultures have a fantastic sense of smell.	

2   What logical inference can be made on the basis of evidence in this passage?

A   Turkey vultures are drawn to the smell of gasoline.

B   Turkey vultures eat things that would be unsafe for most other animals or people.

C   Turkey vultures prefer animals that have only been dead a short time.

D   Turkey vultures have no natural enemies to threaten them.

3   In what paragraph do you find the evidence to disprove a myth about turkey vultures mentioned in paragraph 1? What is the myth and what evidence disproves it?

_____

_____

_____

_____

4 Why do you think that the author doesn't argue the fact that many people think that turkey vultures are ugly?

_____

_____

_____

_____

 5 Explain in a paragraph why you think the author says that turkey vultures make the world "a nicer place to live." What evidence in the passage supports this opinion? Discuss your response with a partner and then make changes to improve your draft. Be sure to include important details and examples.

RI.4.1	Refer to details and examples in a text when explaining what the text says explicitly and when drawing inferences from the text.
SL.4.1	Engage effectively in a range of collaborative discussions with diverse partners on grade 4 topics and texts, building on others' ideas and expressing their own clearly.
	a. Come to discussions prepared, having read or studied required material; explicitly draw on that preparation and other information known about the topic to explore ideas under discussion.
W.4.2	Write informative/explanatory texts to examine a topic and convey ideas and information clearly.
	a. Introduce a topic clearly and group related information in paragraphs and sections; include formatting, illustrations, and multimedia when useful to aiding comprehension.
CCR.R.1	Read closely to determine what the text says explicitly and to make logical inferences from it; cite specific textual evidence when writing or speaking to support conclusions drawn from the text.

Understand the Standards

In a conversation, two or more people take turns talking and listening. It would be a boring conversation if only one person talked! You may be surprised to learn that when you read information texts, it's also assumed that you will take an **active**, which means an involved or energetic, part in the learning process. You do this by thinking out loud with a partner, on paper, or to yourself about what you are reading. For example, say that you are reading about animals that seem to sense when a big storm is coming. You do much more than read strings of words. Instead:

> **Words to Know**
> active
> background knowledge

○ *You ask questions as you read* as a way to interact with and better comprehend what you're reading.

   Is there any scientific evidence to prove that many animals can predict storms?

○ *You recall your own experience* and **background knowledge,** or what you already know about something, to figure out what the author is talking about.

   I remember my grandpa telling me how he always knew when a storm was coming because the seagulls would leave the coast and fly inland!

○ *You "read between the lines"* to make inferences based on what you know + what you read.

   The author says that animals and birds survived the tsunami in Thailand in 2004 by running to the hills before the huge waves hit the beach. There may be other explanations. I wonder what evidence the author presents.

There is one smart reason for being actively involved as a reader:

Reading + Thinking + Asking Questions As You Read = Good Comprehension

It's also much more fun to read when you're aware of and actively involved in the process. Try it!

Guided Instruction

As you read this piece of informational writing about learning a second language, be an active reader. Think about what the author is saying as you read, and don't be afraid to take notes! Some students like writing their comments and questions on sticky notes.

Multicultural Connection

Learning a Second Language

Learning a second language at any age has its benefits. However, researchers believe that learning a second language as a child has many advantages. For one thing, children who learn a second language gain confidence as learners. They often become excited about learning in general. It increases the "gray matter" in the brain, which is the part of the brain responsible for processing information.

Children are good at mimicking what they hear. Researchers believe this is why children have an easier time picking up the sound of a second language and speaking it smoothly. It also seems to help them develop a bigger vocabulary in their first language. They learn to compare and contrast sentence construction in English, for example, with another language. It also trains their ears to listen for subtle differences in pronunciation.

Learning another language also helps students develop a global awareness. They learn to appreciate other countries and cultures. It allows them to communicate with people they would not otherwise be able to speak with. If they have relatives who speak the language they are learning, they have a way to learn about the memories, traditions, and stories that are a part of that person's life and history.

As students move through school, they have a head start in meeting language requirements in high school and college. Later, it also opens up opportunities in jobs and careers where a second language is a real asset.

Guided Questions

If you had a chance to learn a second language, which one would you pick? Why?

_____

_____

_____

_____

_____

What do you think is the writer's most convincing argument that someone your age should learn a second language?

_____

_____

_____

_____

What personal questions about language might you ask the writer?

_____

_____

_____

_____

Practice being an active reader as you reread the passage and answer the questions below. Hints for thinking about and answering questions are given in parentheses.

1. What new question do you have about the information in paragraph 1?

(Hint: Pretend that the passage is one-half of a conversation. Ask yourself: What questions do I have in response to things the author says?)

_____

_____

_____

2. What background knowledge (a memory, personal experience, or something you learned previously) can you recall that helps you to relate to paragraph 3 or 4?

(Hint: You have a lot of knowledge and have had many experiences. Connect what you already know in some way with everything you read. It will help you understand what you're reading and make it easier to remember later.)

_____

_____

_____

_____

3. What inference can you make based on the information in paragraph 1?

(Hint: Making inferences uses what the author says and what you already know to make sense of what you read.)

_____

_____

_____

_____

On Your Own

As you read this passage, remember to make inferences, ask questions, and connect what you read with your own experience and firsthand knowledge. Then explain to your partner how being an active reader helps your comprehension.

Real World Connection

Soap, Beautiful Soap!

The invention of soap dates back about 2,800 years. For centuries, people used combinations of animal fats and plant or wood ash to make soap. For a long time, soap was primarily used for washing linens and clothes, not bodies.

Since people didn't use soap to wash themselves, bodies tended to smell! People wore little sachets (pouches) of fragrant herbs around their necks or carried them in their pockets. When baths were taken, everyone in the family often bathed in the same tub of water. Children were last, which led to the old saying "Don't throw the baby out with the bathwater!"

The first theory about germs causing disease wasn't published until 1890. Bars of cheap soap became available for the average person to buy at around the same time. People began to see a connection between cleanliness and health.

Today, children learn early on about the importance of washing their hands often and well to keep from spreading germs and getting sick! The next time you wash your hands, be thankful for soap.

Answer the questions based on the passage.

1   What inference can you make from the old saying in paragraph 2? Explain your answer using evidence from the passage.

_____

_____

_____

_____

_____

2 What part do you think wood and plant ash played in making early soaps useful? Use your own background knowledge as well as evidence in the text in your answer.

_____

_____

_____

3 Which statement adds evidence to the information in paragraph 3?

A Detergents are used to get laundry clean, but they contain chemical ingredients instead of soap.

B In 1861, a Hungarian doctor wrote a book about the importance of doctors washing their hands in hospitals, but many doctors thought it was too much work.

C Ivory Soap, the "soap that floats," was made by accident in 1879 when a worker forgot to shut off a machine and too much air was added to the soap mixture.

D Many soaps made now are biodegradable, which means they can break down easily in the environment without harming our rivers and streams.

4 In which paragraph would this statement fit best?

To help children wash their hands long enough, they are encouraged to sing the "Happy Birthday" song.

A paragraph 1

B paragraph 4

C paragraph 3

D paragraph 2

5 If you learned that, like wood ash, wet clay and wet sand were also used in making soap long ago, what inference would you make about all three substances?

_____

_____

_____

6 Why do you think it took so long for ordinary people to use soap to clean their bodies?

_____

_____

_____

_____

_____

Critical Thinking

7 On a separate piece of paper, and using pictures as well as words if desired, work with a partner to create a new innovation that you would like to see in soap. Begin by writing a report. You and your partner can divide the topic into parts, with each of you taking different parts. Remember to group your ideas logically in paragraphs and sections. Use headings to organize your information clearly. Then present your report to the class and explain why your idea would be useful or popular. Use illustrations, diagrams, and even short videos to make your presentation interesting.

RI.4.2	Determine the main idea of a text and explain how it is supported by key details; summarize the text.
SL.4.1	Engage effectively in a range of collaborative discussions with diverse partners on grade 4 topics and texts, building on others' ideas and expressing their own clearly. **d.** Review the key ideas expressed and explain their own ideas and understanding in light of the discussion.
W.4.2	Write informative/explanatory texts to examine a topic and convey ideas and information clearly. **e.** Provide a concluding statement or section related to the information or explanation presented.
CCR.R.2	Determine central ideas or themes of a text and analyze their development; summarize the key supporting details and ideas.

Understand the Standards

Real World Connection

Whether you are reading for information as part of a school report or as part of a job as an adult, there is a lot of information to wade through! Good readers develop **strategies**, or tactics, to use to quickly figure out what the main idea of a piece of writing is about.

Words to Know

strategies

headline

subtitle

introductory or
  concluding paragraph

- In newspapers, magazine articles, books, and films, the **headline** (the title of a newspaper article), title, and **subtitle** (the second, more descriptive title of a book or article, often separated from the main title by a colon) provide clues about the content of the piece of writing. Good writers read the title and ask themselves: *What does this article or book seem to be about?*

Example: (magazine article) "Sleep-Deprived or Spoiled?: The Debate on Delayed School Start Times for Middle and High School Students"

- Good readers pay close attention to the first and last paragraphs in a chapter, paragraph, or section of a book for clues as to what the writing is about. The main idea of a piece of writing often appears in the **introductory or concluding paragraph**. This means that the author may *introduce* the passage by telling readers what will be covered or *end* the passage by summarizing what was said.

Example: (introduction) Parents, teachers, students, and researchers differ in their opinions about the best starting time for school for middle school students. This article explores the pros and cons of delaying school start times to allow students more hours of sleep.

Guided Instruction

As you read this piece of informational writing about the starting time for school, set a good example and stay awake! Ask questions as you read and try to identify how the author organizes this piece of writing.

Sleep-Deprived or Spoiled?:
The Debate on Delayed School Start Times
for Middle and High School Students

It's 7 A.M. on Monday, a school day. Still, if you are in middle (or high school) in many school districts around the country, you can stay in bed for an extra hour. No one even minds! Your school decided there was evidence to support delaying the start of the school day. Instead of arriving as early as 7:30 A.M., school won't start until 8:45 A.M.

Researchers believe that this extra time for sleep helps teens in several ways. They say it seems to promote better sleep, increased motivation, and a better overall mood. They base their argument on adolescents' changing sleep patterns. This changing pattern makes it hard for teens to fall asleep before 11 P.M., even though they still need at least nine hours of sleep each night.

Educators who have experienced later start times in their schools reported that students performed better, had improved grades in their first two class periods, and seemed more alert. It also seems to decrease tardiness, fatigue, and illness. On the down side, families have to adjust their morning schedules and carpooling routines. After-school activities such as sports are delayed due to a later school day. This can pose problems, especially during the winter darkness. It also interferes with high school students who need after-school jobs.

Guided Questions

What is the "big idea," or central idea, that this passage is promoting?

_____

_____

_____

After introducing the topic, what are the three main points the writer makes?

_____

_____

_____

_____

_____

_____

_____

Why do you think the writer started with research first?

_____

_____

_____

_____

_____

In many districts, everyone came to like the change, and it will continue this year. Some districts solved the problem of athletic competition schedules by allowing students to leave school early on those days. Other districts will be watching the data from these schools carefully. By the time you enter middle school, you may be sleeping later, too!

Guided Questions

How convincing is the conclusion? What would you add?

_____

_____

_____

_____

Answer and discuss these questions about the passage.

1. Where would you advise readers to look first to get an idea of the main idea of this passage?

_____

_____

_____

_____

2. What detail in the title and subtitle isn't really part of an argument in the passage?

_____

_____

_____

_____

3. If you were to add some new information to this piece of writing in the form of a new paragraph, what would you like to add, and where would you insert it in the passage?

_____

_____

_____

_____

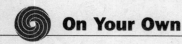

On Your Own

Read the passage, then complete the activities.

Travelin' Shoes

How do *you* get from place to place? You'd probably say by foot, bike, bus, or car. Now imagine being a seed. With none of those options readily available, seeds need other means of transportation. The interesting part is that you know they find a way, because seeds spring up all over your yard, in the vacant lot in your neighborhood, and even in unlikely places where no one has seen them before.

Many seeds are planted by farmers or by anyone else with a backyard or window garden. Seeds from these plants may be saved and given to someone else to plant. Other seeds, however, depend on nature to help them find a home far away from their parent plant.

Some seeds depend on their shape and size to help them travel. The whirlybird seeds released from maple trees look like miniature helicopters. Their lightweight, papery wings and sleek shape allow them to be easily picked up and carried by the wind to new locations. Other seeds, like dandelions, resemble parachutes. Their fluffy clusters of seeds also rely on the wind to blow them to new places.

Other seeds have a sticky texture or little spikes and barbs. These features help them to hop a ride on things such as your pant leg, your shoelaces, or your dog's fur. You or your dog march them out of their original environment and into a new place!

Some seeds depend on animals to help them in their travels. Sometimes animals eat a fruit such as an apple and later leave the waste product, including seeds, in a new location. Other times animals like squirrels may bury an acorn and not return to get it.

Some seeds float downstream in a river, washing up on a shore far from home. If conditions are right, they might begin to grow there. Some floating seeds are tiny, but some large seeds like coconuts can float!

Complete the following activities based on the passage you just read.

1 What kinds of details does the author mainly include in this passage?

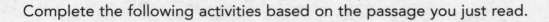

_____

_____

2 What question do you have after reading paragraph 6?

_____

_____

_____

3 Which answer best summarizes the role of nature in how seeds travel?

A Nature protects seeds until they find a good place to grow.

B Seeds travel with the help of wind, water, animals, and humans.

C Wind and water are undependable means of travel for seeds.

D Some seeds have barbs or spikes that enable them to stick to fabric or fur.

4 What key detail does the author expect readers to infer from this statement?

Other times animals like squirrels may bury an acorn and not return to get it.

A Many of the seeds are wasted by squirrels.

B Some of the buried acorn seeds will start to grow.

C Most animals disperse seeds within a short distance of their homes.

D All animals help seeds disperse in some way.

5 Why do you think it's important for seeds to grow far away from parent plants?

_____

_____

_____

_____

_____

6 This passage lacks a formal conclusion and just seems to end "up in the air." Write a formal concluding paragraph. Summarize this passage in your own words and add some final thoughts.

 7 Work with a partner to discuss the various ways the article tells how seeds are spread. Then answer this question: On the basis of what you've read, what part do you think birds play in how seeds travel? Explain your thoughts in a short paragraph.

RI.4.5	Describe the overall structure of events, ideas, concepts, or information in a text or part of a text.
SL.4.2	Paraphrase portions of a text read aloud or information presented in diverse media and formats, including visually, quantitatively, and orally.
W.4.1	Write opinion pieces on topics or texts, supporting a point of view with reasons and information. **b.** Provide reasons that are supported by facts and details.
CCR.R.5	Analyze the structure of texts, including how specific sentences, paragraphs, and larger portions of the text relate to each other and the whole.

Understand the Standards

When reading nonfiction, you often skip around because you want to find specific information. Different types of nonfiction are divided into chunks that are called by different names.

> **Words to Know**
> sections
> scenes
> stanza
> refrain

- Books are divided into paragraphs. The paragraphs make up chapters. The chapters may be grouped into larger **sections**.

  For example, in a book on United States history, the Table of Contents tells you that Section 4: World War II has six chapters. If you want information on women's changing roles during World War II, you will likely find it in Section 4.

- Plays are divided into sections called acts, which are then divided into **scenes**. Scenes tell you who is on stage and where and when the action takes place.

  Example: Act I, Scene 1: *June 1922. A lonely café in the middle of the desert. A rusted red truck sits out front. A few items of laundry hang out an upstairs window, stiff as the fateful wind that blew Cal toward the café's rickety screen door.*

- Music and poetry are often divided into sections called **stanzas** that share qualities of line length, meter, rhyme, or number of lines. Some poems have a **refrain**, one or more lines that repeat at regular intervals, especially at the end of verses. Below is an example of a triplet, or three-line stanza.

  Example: *Pine needles rained down*
  Punctuating our perfect picnic
  With small sticky-tipped spears.

  We transformed into tiny trees
  Branches poking from our hair
  A miniature forest family of five.

Guided Instruction

Here are the first three stanzas of a famous 17-stanza poem. Read it once to yourself and then again softly out loud.

from **The Highwayman**
by Alfred Noyes

The wind was a torrent of darkness among the gusty trees,
The moon was a ghostly galleon tossed upon cloudy seas,
The road was a ribbon of moonlight over the purple moor,
And the highwayman came riding—
Riding—riding—
The highwayman came riding, up to the old inn door.

He'd a French cocked hat on his forehead, a bunch of lace at
   his chin,
A coat of the claret velvet, and breeches of brown doe-skin;
They fitted with never a wrinkle: his boots were up to the thigh!
And he rode with a jeweled twinkle,
His pistol butts a-twinkle—
His rapier hilts a-twinkle, under the jeweled sky.

Over the cobbles he clattered and clashed in the dark inn-yard,
And he tapped with his whip on the shutters, but all was locked
   and barred;
He whistled a tune to the window, and who should be waiting there
But the landlord's black-eyed daughter,
Bess, the landlord's daughter,
Plaiting a dark red love-knot into her long black hair.

Guided Questions

What images or ideas does the first stanza focus on?

_____

_____

_____

_____

_____

_____

What impression does it create in your mind?

_____

_____

What images or ideas does the second stanza focus on?

_____

_____

_____

What impression does it create in your mind?

_____

_____

_____

Complete the following activities.

1. What images or ideas does the third stanza focus on?

_____

_____

2. Think about your answer to the previous question and the ones in the margins of the poem. Describe the relationship between stanzas and idea or images.

_____

_____

_____

3. In your own words, describe what a stanza is. How can you tell where one stanza ends and the next one begins?

_____

_____

_____

_____

4. What can you guess about the organization of the poem based on the first three stanzas? What happens in these stanzas?

_____

_____

_____

5. What do scenes, paragraphs and sections, and stanzas have in common?

_____

_____

_____

_____

_____

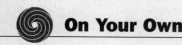

On Your Own

The song "Grandfather's Clock" was written in 1876. It was so popular that longcase clocks like the one in the song became known as *grandfather clocks*.

Music/Arts
Connection

from **Grandfather's Clock**
by Henry Clay Work

My grandfather's clock was too tall for the shelf
So it stood ninety years on the floor.
It was taller by half than the old man himself
Though it weighed not a pennyweight more
It was bought on the morn of the day that he was born
And was always his treasure and pride.
But it stopped, short, never to go again
When the old man died

> *Ninety years without slumbering*
> *(Tick tock tick tock)*
> *His life's seconds numbering*
> *(Tick tock tick tock)*
> *It stopped, short, never to go again*
> *When the old man died.*

In watching its pendulum swing to and fro
Many hours he had spent when a boy
And through childhood and manhood, the clock seemed to know
And to share both his grief and his joy
For it struck 24 when he entered at the door
With a blooming and beautiful bride,
But it stopped, short, never to go again
When the old man died

> *[Refrain]*

My grandfather said that of those he could hire
Not a servant so faithful he'd found,
For it kept perfect time and it had one desire
At the close of each day to be wound
And it kept to its place, not a frown upon its face
And its hands never hung by its side
But it stopped, short, never to go again
When the old man died

> *[Refrain]*

Complete the following activities based on the passage you just read.

Elevate **1** Analyze the organization and progression of this song.

_____

_____

_____

_____

_____

_____

2 How would you explain the purpose of the refrain and especially the repeating "tick tock tick tock" in this song?

_____

_____

_____

_____

3 A paragraph in a book is most similar to a _____ in a song.

A refrain

B stanza

C scene

D section

4 Which answer best describes why the analogy continued in stanza 6 works so well?

A The words *place/face* and *side/died* rhyme.

B The poet continues to use the pronouns *it* and *its* in lines 1 and 2.

C The same words are used to describe both a person's body and a clock.

D The changing rhythm of the lines takes readers by surprise.

5 Why do you think the grandfather starts talking about the clock as a person toward the end of his life?

_____

_____

_____

Discuss

6 Discuss with a partner why you think the song is so effective in painting a picture of the relationship between a valued object and its owner. Is there anything else that, in your opinion, has made this song so beloved over time? Evaluate the soundness of each other's arguments and what, if anything, could make them stronger.

_____

_____

_____

_____

_____

_____

Elevate **7** Reread the lyrics of "Grandfather's Clock" again. On a separate piece of paper, discuss how the song describes what the grandfather valued at different stages in his life. Remember to include evidence from the song, including paraphrases of various verses, to support your ideas. Illustrate your report when you are done.

RI.4.3	Explain events, procedures, ideas, or concepts in a historical, scientific, or technical text, including what happened and why, based on specific information in the text.
SL.4.4	Report on a topic or text, tell a story, or recount an experience in an organized manner, using appropriate facts and relevant, descriptive details to support main ideas or themes; speak clearly at an understandable pace.
W.4.1	Write opinion pieces on topics or texts, supporting a point of view with reasons and information. **a.** Introduce a topic or text clearly, state an opinion, and create an organizational structure in which related ideas are grouped to support the writer's purpose.
CCR.R.3	Analyze how and why individuals, events, and ideas develop and interact over the course of the text.

Understand the Standards

When you **paraphrase**, you explain something in your own words, focusing on the most important points. You paraphrase every time you tell a friend about the show you saw. You pick out the most important things and tell them in your own words.

> **Words to Know**
> paraphrase
> plagiarism

Good readers learn to paraphrase (out loud with a partner or to themselves) as they read or listen as a way to check their own comprehension. If you can stop after a page, a paragraph, a section of a book or article, or a presentation and paraphrase it in your own words, you know you understood what you read. What's more, just knowing you are going to ask yourself to do that helps train you to stay aware and actively participate as you read! You begin to build a habit of asking questions, identifying evidence, and linking what you are learning with your own background knowledge and personal experience.

Here's how it works. I just finished reading the two paragraphs about paraphrasing. Now my partner and I are going to take turns paraphrasing what we read to see how much we understood:

> Those two paragraphs talked about the importance of taking the time to paraphrase, or say what you read in your own words. If I do that, I can build a habit of thinking about what I'm reading, asking questions in my mind, and relating it to things I already know.

After taking turns, my partner and I both know we understood what we read because we could say it in our own words, so we continue on.

Paraphrasing is especially helpful when you read informational books or articles, because it helps you keep track of events and ideas that change over time. Making it a habit to paraphrase also helps you to avoid **plagiarism**, or copying someone else's words and using them as your own, when you write. When you use someone's words, you must signal that they aren't yours by using quotation marks and telling whose words they are. Paraphrasing solves that problem.

Guided Instruction

Have you ever dissected an owl pellet? Here's how. Read this passage carefully, thinking carefully about what you are reading.

Science Connection

Owl Pellets

Owls are raptors that swallow their prey whole or nearly whole. Owls produce small round pellets that are composed of the undigested bones, fur, teeth, and hair of the animal that was eaten. Owls regurgitate, or throw up, one small round pellet about 20 hours after eating.

Dissecting, or carefully taking apart, an owl pellet tells you many things. It tells you what the owl ate, what animals are in the owl's habitat, and what an owl can and cannot digest.

Some classes purchase owl pellets for students to dissect. For safety reasons, it's important to wear gloves, because the pellets may contain bacteria. You also need tweezers and some simple dissecting tools. You'll also need a small bowl of water and sheets with drawings of the bones of several different rodent skeletons.

Carefully pick up the owl pellet and look at the outside of it. You might want to use a jeweler's loupe to get a close-up look. What do you see? What does it tell you? Make some notes on your observations.

Now, begin to carefully squeeze the pellet to gently break it apart. Use the tweezers and picks to expose and pull out each bone you find. Wash off each bone in the bowl of water and carefully set it aside.

When you have found all the bones, teeth, and anything else of interest in your owl pellet, study the skeleton drawings of different rodents. Which one matches your bones? After you identify the rodent skeleton in your owl pellet, pretend you're working on a jigsaw puzzle. Place each bone on the skeleton drawing and see how many you can match up. What bones did you find? What ones are missing?

When you are finished, do a drawing of your skeleton. Explain the procedure in your own words. Write a list of assumptions you can make based on the evidence. What remaining questions do you have?

Guided Questions

Give yourself an overview. What is the overall purpose of each paragraph?

_____

_____

_____

_____

_____

_____

_____

_____

_____

_____

How can knowing the purpose of a paragraph help you paraphrase the contents?

_____

_____

_____

_____

Complete the following activities.

1. Describe the structure of "Owl Pellets."

_____

_____

2. Paraphrase the process of dissecting an owl pellet. Then explain why you might not want to rely on paraphrased information.

_____

_____

_____

_____

_____

_____

3. How do you think owl pellets provide clues about the owl's habitat?

_____

_____

_____

_____

 Measuring Up® to the New York Common Core

On Your Own

This science article connects information that may be new to you with information you already know. Think about each paragraph as you read. Analyze how the author structured this piece of writing and how the ideas developed.

The Inside Story

Skeletons are important. They provide the scaffolding for a sturdy new house, the framework for a protective bike helmet, or the outline for your next research project.

Human builders have often copied designs from the plant and animal world. Think of how much curved stone bridges resemble the backs of elephants. Have you ever noticed how the shape of the Eiffel Tower has a lot in common with the shape of a giraffe? What other examples can you think of?

Hollow construction can be seen in everything from vegetables to old buildings to bird bones. Cut into a green pepper and notice the hollowed-out construction. Many paper lanterns use a similar design. Hollow construction makes a lot of sense when you don't want to add extra weight but need the support. The ancient Romans placed empty clay pots and pumice in the concrete when pouring the domes and walls of many ancient buildings.

Bird skeletons are highly adapted for flight. Most birds have many bones that are hollow with criss-crossing pieces for added strength. Birds' hollow bones are very lightweight but strong enough to withstand the physical stress of taking off, flying, and landing. The number of hollow bones varies, depending on the species. Large birds that glide and soar tend to have the greatest number of hollow bones. Some birds, like ostriches and penguins, have solid bones.

The next time you are out in nature, observe the structures of the plants and animals you see. Ask yourself: What function does that structure serve? What does it remind me of?

Complete the following activities.

1   How are birds built to fly? Explain in your own words, using information from the passage.

_____

_____

_____

_____

2   Based on information in this passage, why don't penguins have hollow bones? What inference might you make?

_____

_____

_____

_____

3   Which answer best paraphrases why skeletal structures are important?

   A Skeletal structures help hold up buildings in any weather.

   B Skeletal structures provide the right support for the job.

   C Skeletal structures give something for skin to attach to.

   D Skeletal structures keep birds from falling from the sky.

4   Why does the author of this passage compare animals and buildings?

   A to make a case for building more curved bridges

   B to prove that many architects can't think of new ideas

   C to show that people get many good ideas from nature

   D to prove that people long ago were behind in their thinking

     Measuring Up® to the New York Common Core

5 How might studying animals that move through tall grass help architects figure out structures built to withstand floods?

_____

_____

_____

_____

_____

_____

_____

6 What new example can you think of where an animal's body and an object are alike in their design?

_____

_____

_____

_____

 7 Working with a partner, analyze in what ways you think human skeletons are built for survival. In what ways could the design be better, in your opinion? Together, produce a report for your class. Use specific examples, including drawings or photos, to explain your ideas clearly. Share your writing orally with the class. Remember to speak clearly and at an appropriate pace.

Lesson 28

Identifying Reasons and Evidence

RI.4.8	Explain how an author uses reasons and evidence to support particular points in a text.
SL.4.5	Add audio recordings and visual displays to presentations when appropriate to enhance the development of main ideas or themes.
W.4.2	Write informative/explanatory texts to examine a topic and convey ideas and information clearly.
	d. Use precise language and domain-specific vocabulary to inform about or explain the topic.
CCR.R.8	Delineate and evaluate the argument and specific claims in a text, including the validity of the reasoning as well as the relevance and sufficiency of the evidence.

Understand the Standards

When you read, an author often has an opinion on the topic. If so, it's important to keep track of the **arguments**, or claims, he or she makes. What reasons are given to support the author's claims? Identifying the reasons and evidence in a piece of informational writing is a good way to be an active reader. It helps you to make sense of and recall what you read.

> **Words to Know**
> arguments
> relevant
> sufficient
> valid

Here are three questions to ask regarding the evidence in a piece of writing:

1. *Is it relevant?*
   If evidence is **relevant**, it pertains to the topic. If an article maintains that a certain type of dog food is best for puppies, but the dog owners quoted all have older dogs, you know the evidence isn't relevant. It doesn't support the main idea.

2. *Is it sufficient?*
   If the evidence is **sufficient**, it means that there is enough evidence to support the author's claim. To prove that "most studies" show that students prefer to work collaboratively, you would need to see the results of a number of different studies. To be convinced that one store in town has the best prices on school supplies, you'd want to compare prices from a number of other stores, not just one.

3. *Is it valid?*
   If the evidence is **valid**, it means that it seems to be true. Many times an author will provide references that tell where he or she got the information. The author may use statistics or other data as proof, or quote a knowledgeable source. Other times, the author's logical reasoning makes the argument seem valid. When you find information on the Internet, it's especially important to know the source.

Writers use precise language and specific topic-related terms to present their arguments and evidence. Look for those terms when you read.

     Measuring Up® to the New York Common Core

Guided Instruction

This informational passage wants to persuade people your age to save money. Read this passage carefully, thinking about the arguments presented. Are they relevant? Are they sufficient? Are they valid? Then answer the questions that follow.

Real World Connection

Develop the Savings Habit!

Some people grow up thinking that they will begin to save money when they have more to save, maybe next month or next year. Sadly for many people, the day to start saving money never comes. It's just too easy to find places to spend money. But, if you do get in the habit of saving even a little money early in life, a number of positive things happen.

First, you get in the savings habit. Banks note that people who begin the habit of saving early in life are more likely to create a lifelong pattern of saving and managing their money. If you get an allowance, you save a little of it every month. If you walk your neighbor's dog, you save one week's worth of the money you earn each month. You might save for something special that you want to buy, or you might just save it to see the money (and interest earned) build up.

Either way you get to see the money you save build up. It doesn't take long for a few dollars to build up to many more dollars. It helps if you have a passbook and get reports on the interest that accrues. If you open a special kids' savings account at your local bank or credit union, you may receive extra prizes and incentives for saving.

Third, you experience the excitement of setting a goal and then reaching it! Say that you want to save $100 for the trip you will take with your grandparents next summer. It seems like a lot of money to save now, but when next summer comes and you have reached your goal, you'll be proud and happy! Your success will also make it that much easier to set a new goal.

Guided Questions

What is the purpose of the opening paragraph? Why might the writer think it is important to say this?

_____

_____

_____

_____

_____

_____

What words and phrases specific to the topic of money and savings do you find in paragraph 2? Why does the writer use them?

_____

_____

_____

_____

_____

When saving money becomes a lifelong habit, you can sustain the practice. Maybe you'll start saving for major things like college, a car, or a house payment. You'll be more likely to save up for big-ticket items instead of borrowing money to buy them.

So start today! Set a goal, start saving even a little, and watch your money grow!

Answer and discuss these questions about the passage. Hints for thinking about and answering questions are given in parentheses.

1. What kind of evidence does the author use?

   (Remember: Asking questions as you read is one way of being an active reader.)

   _____

   _____

   _____

   _____

   _____

2. In your opinion, was the evidence presented relevant, sufficient, and valid enough?

   (Hint: Ask yourself whether you're convinced. Think about what added evidence would convince you.)

   _____

   _____

   _____

   _____

   _____

   _____

On Your Own

The author uses reasoning as well as facts to explain details about a creature of the deep ocean. Think about each paragraph as you read. Pay attention to the evidence presented, new questions you may have, and inferences you can make.

Science Connection

Creatures of the Deep: Giant Tube Worms

You may be familiar with the ocean, but very few people have seen what some scientists have discovered in the deep ocean. "Deep ocean" means at least a mile down. It's so far from the surface that no sunlight reaches these depths. The water pressure has been compared to having 50 gigantic airplanes stacked on top of you! If you had the courage and the right equipment, you could be among the first to explore at these depths.

About one mile deep on the Pacific Ocean floor, volcanic thermal vents spew chemicals. Few animals could survive in such a harsh, toxic environment. Scientists were surprised to find whole ecosystems living amid the boiling-hot chemical soup of acids and gases around these vents, including giant tube worms.

These huge creatures can reach over eight feet in length. Their plumes reach frigid water that is just above freezing. The bottom of the worm stands in hot water. They live their lives in utter darkness without oxygen. They have no eyes. They don't have a mouth or a digestive system either. Instead, they use bacteria inside them to meet their energy needs. Their distinctive red plumes supply nutrients to the bacteria inside them. They also provide a tasty snack for the shrimp and crab that nibble off bits of the plumes.

Thanks to researchers and new technologies that include submersibles, cameras, and other tools, thousands of new species like the giant tube worm have been identified in the deep ocean. Scientists say that it is by far the largest habitat for life on Earth. At present it is also the most unknown area of the sea.

Answer the questions based on the passage.

1 What comparison does the author use to help readers understand the pressure of the water at one mile deep?

_____

_____

_____

_____

2 On the basis of the evidence in this passage, why do you think giant tube worms have no eyes, mouth, or digestive system? What inference and new question might you make about other species?

_____

_____

_____

_____

_____

_____

_____

_____

_____

3 According to the passage, what flows out of thermal vents deep in the ocean?

   A deep-ocean creatures without eyes

   B toxic chemicals, acids, and gases

   C many kinds of bacteria

   D giant red plumes full of nutrients

4 What surprised scientists about deep-ocean life around the vents?

   A Thick toxic soup oozes out and covers everything.

   B Vents allow scientists to explore underwater volcanoes.

   C Whole ecosystems live around these toxic deep-ocean vents.

   D Bacteria may be hazardous to scientists exploring the area.

5 What evidence convinces you that it isn't easy to survive in the deep ocean?

_____

_____

_____

_____

_____

_____

_____

_____

Critical Thinking

6 Work with a partner. On a separate piece of paper, each of you should analyze what you would like the author to cover in a follow-up article on the subject. Tell what you would like to know about in more detail and what new related topics the author might explore. Then combine your two papers. Choose the best parts of each. Make sure the final paper makes sense. After you are done, present your suggestions to the class. Find and use some audiovisual materials, including photographs and videos from the Web, that would add interest to your presentation.

RI.4.7	Interpret information presented visually, orally, or quantitatively, and explain how the information contributes to an understanding of the text in which it appears.
SL.4.5	Add audio recordings and visual displays to presentations when appropriate to enhance the development of main ideas or themes.
W.4.2	Write informative/explanatory texts to examine a topic and convey ideas and information clearly. **a.** Introduce a topic clearly and group related information in paragraphs and sections; include formatting, illustrations, and multimedia when useful to aiding comprehension.
CCR.R.7	Integrate and evaluate content presented in diverse media and formats, including visually and quantitatively, as well as in words.

Understand the Standards

Have you ever heard the expression "A picture is worth a thousand words"? This old saying reminds us that sometimes one good **graphic**—a visual image, such as a photo, illustration, chart, or graph—can say something more concisely and fully than words alone.

When we learn something, we usually use more than one of our senses. If your dad barbecues something, he may say, "It's burger time," but the smell and sizzling sound of them cooking make his words come to life in a much more vivid way. If you study the events leading up to the Revolutionary War, your social studies book explains the details in words, but if you also see a visual **time line**, a linear chronological list of important events; a painting of the Boston Tea Party; or a reenactment of the Boston Tea Party, it helps bring to life that period in history. When we can connect more than one of our senses to what we are learning, it makes an impression and helps us recall the details.

Which of these do you think would be the most memorable?

- hearing an **audio**, or sound, recording of Dr. Martin Luther King Jr.'s "I Have a Dream" speech

- reading the words of the actual speech

- watching a **video**, or movie, recording of Dr. King delivering the "I Have a Dream" speech

If you said watching a video recording, you'd be right. You would see Dr. King, hear his words, and could read the text of his speech later. But, what you gain in that format is even more than the speech. You can observe the crowd that's present, feel the excitement, and see the Lincoln Memorial and other parts of the National Mall that memorable August day in 1963.

Guided Instruction

Here is a short passage about types of clouds. As you read, note how the visuals enhance your interest in and understanding of this subject.

Science Connection

It's Cloudy!
High-Altitude Clouds

Cirrus

The word *cirrus* literally means "curl of hair" because they look like mare's tails in the sky. These clouds are so high up in the sky that they are made of ice crystals and not drops of water. Cirrus clouds often signal that bad weather is coming.

Low Clouds

Stratus

The word *stratus* means "layers" in Latin. Usually you see stratus clouds as a blanket of gray. They are often part of rainy, drizzly days. When stratus clouds rest on the ground, we call it fog.

Clouds with Vertical Growth

Cumulus

Cumulus means "heap." These big puffy clouds look like balls of cotton. Children often see pictures in these clouds. They usually appear in fair weather when the sky is blue.

Storm Clouds

Cumulonimbus

Nimbus means "rain." These big black thunderhead clouds appear when rain is coming.

Guided Questions

When you started to read this passage, did you look at the illustrations first or go straight to the text? Why?

_____

_____

_____

_____

How accurately do the photographs represent the verbal descriptions in the text?

_____

_____

_____

_____

Which photograph was the most effective? Why?

_____

_____

_____

_____

Answer and discuss these questions about the passage.

1. What does the author of this passage use to get across the information?

_____

_____

_____

_____

2. In your opinion, what would you have missed if the illustrations had not been included?

_____

_____

_____

_____

3. What other similar topic would be much more useful if pictures were added?

_____

_____

_____

_____

 On Your Own

As you read this time line of events leading up to the American Revolution, think about how a time line gives information as compared to reading a chapter in a textbook.

 Time Line of Events Leading to the American Revolution

The American Revolution resulted from a chain of events. As Great Britain tried to levy more taxes on the upstart colonies, the colonies responded with anger at the unfair treatment and "taxation without representation." Thus began a growing desire by colonists to be free from rule by England. This time line shows some of the main events leading to the American Revolution.

1754–1763

The French and Indian War
This long and costly war left Great Britain heavily in debt. Taxing the colonies would help raise money to repay this debt.

1764

The Sugar Act
This act put a three-cent tax on sugar, which angered colonial merchants.

1765

The Stamp Act
This tax on pamphlets, newspapers, and other documents was the first direct tax on the colonists.

1767

The Townshend Acts
New items used by the colonists were taxed, such as glass, oil, paint, and tea. After colonial protests, Britain eventually repealed all of them but the tax on tea.

1770

The Boston Massacre
The shooting of five colonists by British troops increased colonists' growing distrust of British soldiers.

1773

The Boston Tea Party
A group of angry colonists dumped all the tea held on British ships in Boston harbor into the water in protest of the tax on tea and other practices by the British.

1774

The Intolerable Acts
This series of laws passed by Parliament was designed to punish the colonists after the Boston Tea Party.

1775

Lexington and Concord
The battles at Lexington and Concord marked the first battles of the Revolutionary War.

Using "Time Line of Events Leading to the American Revolution" and what you have learned about time lines in general, complete the following activities.

1 What were colonists paying taxes on directly as of 1765, and how did this differ from earlier taxes?

_____

_____

_____

2 What thread do you see running through this time line in terms of decision making regarding the colonies?

_____

_____

_____

_____

3 Where would you add the Declaratory Act of 1766 on the time line?

A after the Boston Massacre and before the Boston Tea Party

B after the Stamp Act and before the Townshend Acts

C after the Sugar Act and before the Stamp Act

D after the Townshend Acts and before the Boston Massacre

4 Which statement explains why Britain's leaders wanted to tax the colonies?

A They wanted the colonies to be less dependent on them.

B They wanted the colonies to be like other British citizens.

C They wanted to get out of debt after the French and Indian War.

D They wanted the colonies to step up and fight for their rights.

5 Why do you think the Boston Massacre increased the level of colonial anger and distrust even more?

_____

_____

_____

_____

6 How can creating your own time line as you read help increase your comprehension?

_____

_____

_____

_____

 7 On a separate piece of paper, create a time line of five or six main events in your life up to this point. Write a sentence after the date that describes each event. Include illustrations to bring your entries to life. Then use all these elements to write your autobiography. Organize it into paragraphs and sections, with headings like "My Earliest Memories," to keep readers on track. Gather audiovisual materials such as favorite toys and recordings of favorite songs to include with your autobiography.

RI.4.6	Compare and contrast a firsthand and secondhand account of the same event or topic; describe the differences in focus and the information provided.
SL.4.1	Engage effectively in a range of collaborative discussions with diverse partners on grade 4 topics and texts, building on others' ideas and expressing their own clearly. **b.** Follow agreed-upon rules for discussions and carry out assigned roles. **e.** Seek to understand and communicate with individuals from different perspectives and cultural backgrounds.
W.4.2	Write informative/explanatory texts to examine a topic and convey ideas and information clearly. **b.** Develop the topic with facts, definitions, concrete details, quotations, or other information and examples related to the topic.
CCR.R.6	Assess how point of view or purpose shapes the content and style of a text.

 ## Understand the Standards

Have you ever witnessed something and then read about it in the paper later? It can seem like a totally different event! You wonder where the person writing the article got his or her information, because you were there and it seemed completely different to you!

Words to Know
firsthand account
secondhand account
point of view

A **firsthand account** is created by a person who was there and produced the oral or written account out of his or her own experience. Firsthand accounts are also called *primary sources*.

A **secondhand account** is made up of information taken or reinterpreted from other sources. Knowing the reference point, or **point of view**, of a piece of writing can shape the content. It helps you to determine if the evidence is believable. Secondhand accounts are also called *secondary sources*.

Firsthand accounts include diaries, letters, photographs, speeches, or interviews produced during an event—for example, a series of letters written by an immigrant traveling through Ellis Island in New York City in the early 1900s. Secondhand accounts include information gathered from other books, articles, or primary sources. For example, a book on the three main cattle trails leading from Texas through Oklahoma into Kansas in the 1800s includes information from many other sources.

Guided Instruction

Compare these two accounts of the same bicycle accident. Think about what information is different in each account and why.

The Bicycle Accident

Firsthand account (from a friend of the bicyclist):

"My friend was just coming down the street when a car came right out and hit him! He wasn't doing anything wrong. We were on our way to the park to meet Mark and Aiden. My friend was bleeding badly! The driver acted like nothing had even happened. It scared me and it ruined my friend's new bike that he got for his birthday last week. I hope he doesn't get in trouble."

Secondhand account (a local newspaper account):

Today White City had its fourth bicycle accident in three days. The bicyclist, 11-year-old Josh Evans, was traveling down the E. 23rd St. hill at a high rate of speed. The driver, 35-year-old Michael Wong, was slowly backing out of his driveway. He didn't see the bicyclist traveling the wrong way on the one-way street. He immediately stopped his vehicle after bumping the bike's fender, called 911, ran over to help get the bicyclist and his bike out of the street, and administered minor first aid to his bleeding knee. Fortunately, the bicyclist was wearing a helmet. No citations were issued to the driver of the vehicle.

Guided Questions

What if there were no heading? How can you tell which passage is the firsthand account and which is the secondhand account?

_____

_____

_____

_____

_____

Think like an investigator as you reread the passages and then answer these questions. Hints and tips are given in parentheses.

1. What is the tone of the firsthand account? From personal experience, why might that tone signal less credible evidence?

   (Hint: Think about the ways in which the purpose of a piece affects its credibility.)

   _____

   _____

   _____

   _____

   _____

   _____

2. What assumptions might you have made if you had read only the firsthand account?

(Tip: To get closer to the truth in anything you read, consider how point of view shapes the content of what you're reading.)

_____

_____

3. What are the positives and negatives of firsthand accounts and secondhand accounts?

(Tip: Remember to be an active reader! Think about the information that's presented and evaluate the point of view. Ask yourself if the evidence seems credible. Do you need to consult more—and different—sources to know for sure?)

_____

_____

_____

_____

_____

_____

_____

_____

On Your Own

As you read these two passages, think about how the voice used in each one influences the lens through which the same period in history is discussed. How does the point of view shape the content?

Arriving at Ellis Island

Multicultural
Connection

Passage 1: Secondhand account

Many people shuffled through the gates, their eyes tired and glazed over. They looked as if they had arrived from another planet and were trying to get their bearings in the bright sunlight of a new land. Imagine how it must have felt to be off the ship after so many days. Children held tightly to their parents' hands. The parents looked around for a familiar face or someone here who spoke their language. Everywhere you looked there were lines packed with people. For many, the two-week voyage was spent in cramped, lower decks packed with countless other men, women, and children, along with the meager belongings they could carry with them to their new home in America. Twelve million immigrants were processed through Ellis Island in New York between 1892 and 1954. It is said that around 50 percent of people living in the United States today can trace at least one family member who immigrated to this country by way of Ellis Island.

Passage 2: Firsthand account

It was 1920. My uncle in New York had bought tickets for my father and me to come to New York, a place much safer than Poland after World War I. We had to leave my mother and two sisters behind. My father said he would save money to send for them later. The voyage was awful. It was dark and cramped in our compartments below the decks, surrounded by hundreds of strangers. I could hardly breathe and would go up on deck to get some fresh air, no matter how stormy the weather was. I got very ill on board the ship. When we reached Ellis Island, a doctor examined everyone on board. No one who was sick could enter the country! My father was free to go, but I was not because I had a cold. I was so scared that I would never see my father again or that I would be sent back to Poland on the ship. I passed the time playing with other boys who were sick, too. Finally, my cold got better and my uncle and father came to get me. I was free at last in my new country, America!

Complete the following activities.

1 What is one fact you learned from the secondhand passage that you would not have known from reading the firsthand account?

_____

_____

2 What, in your opinion, was the best part about reading the firsthand passage?

_____

_____

_____

3 If you wanted to find out about the history of Ellis Island, you would want to consult

A a primary source.

B a secondary source.

C a firsthand account.

D a book of diary entries.

4 A firsthand account is not always 100 reliable as a reference because

A people often share their accounts with other people before writing them down.

B how someone sees an event can be influenced by things such as surprise, shock, or fear.

C it is based on the reports and research of other people and not on one person's real experiences.

D all firsthand accounts are recalled long after the event is over when memories have faded.

5 How do the two passages on Ellis Island give readers a better picture of that time and place than either passage alone could do? Follow agreed-upon rules in a class discussion on the topic.

_____

_____

_____

_____

_____

6 In what way might primary source materials be helpful to someone writing a secondhand account on the same subject? Illustrate your point with an example from the passages.

_____

_____

_____

_____

7 Ellis Island is now closed and has become a museum. Work with a small group to discuss how people enter the United States today. Invite them to do an oral history project with willing older relatives and family friends. Have group members gather stories and memories from one older adult to share with the group. If possible, have the group work in teams to do interviews. Have subjects tell how they felt when they first arrived. Interviews will vary.

8 Imagine that you and two partners are researching space travel. Work together to prepare and present a classroom discussion about your topic. Begin by listing on a sheet of paper at least three different types of sources you might use. What kind of information would you expect to find in each one? Next, for class, decide on rules for the discussion. Then, choose one of you to act as moderator and have the other two present the topic and answer questions. At the end, discuss how effective the discussion was.

RI.4.9	Integrate information from two texts on the same topic in order to write or speak about the subject knowledgeably.
SL.4.1	Engage effectively in a range of collaborative discussions with diverse partners on grade 4 topics and texts, building on others' ideas and expressing their own clearly.
	c. Pose and respond to specific questions to clarify or follow up on information, and make comments that contribute to the discussion and link to the remarks of others.
W.4.3	Write narratives to develop real or imagined experiences or events using effective technique, descriptive details, and clear event sequences.
	d. Use concrete words and phrases and sensory details to convey experiences and events precisely.
CCR.R.9	Analyze how two or more texts address similar themes or topics in order to build knowledge or to compare the approaches the authors take.

Understand the Standards

Researching a topic is a lot like the old familiar folktale "The Blind Men and the Elephant." In this folktale, the blind men all touched a different part of the elephant. Each man assumed that the elephant must look like the tiny part he touched, such as the tail or a tusk. It was only when they all pooled their ideas that they could come up with an accurate idea of what an elephant might be like.

Words to Know
assumptions
perspectives

Sports Connection

In the same way, when you research a topic, you don't want to make **assumptions**, or conclusions, based on one source that just gives you one small piece of the puzzle. You want to consider many **perspectives**, meaning points of view or angles, on the subject. Before you even begin, take some time to increase your background knowledge. This will help you identify and narrow down your own topic. Take a subject like baseball. You could talk about

- the history of the sport

- famous Hall of Fame baseball players

- rules of the game

- changes in uniforms through the ages

- the Negro Leagues

- the minor league team in your hometown

- collecting baseball cards

- the history of how wooden bats are made

After you review a few sources, it will be easier to choose a topic that is interesting to you. As you write, make sure you consult several sources so that you have a variety of opinions and perspectives on the topic.

Guided Instruction

Compare these excerpts from two sources on the Negro Leagues. Think about how each of them is valuable in gaining knowledge of the subject.

History Connection

The Negro Leagues

Today baseball teams have players representing many ethnic groups. But it was not always that way. For a long time, African American players were banned from playing in the major and minor leagues. Finally, they started their own leagues.

The first Negro League, the Negro National League, operated from 1920 until 1931. Just as with the white major leagues, the Negro Leagues had their own World Series every year. In addition, in 1933, the African American teams began to play an all-star competition in Chicago each summer known as the East-West game. This game was more popular than the World Series and attracted as many as 50,000 people.

Jackie Robinson

Jackie Robinson played with the Negro Leagues but broke the color barrier when he played his first game with the all-white Montreal Royals, a Brooklyn Dodgers farm team, in 1945. It was a hard year. People in the stands sometimes jeered him, and Jackie and his family received threats.

After one season in Montreal, Jackie Robinson joined the Dodgers. There were more threats, and even members of his own team threatened to sit out in protest of having him on the team. The manager remained loyal to Jackie, however, which helped set a good example for the other players and teams. In his first year on the team, Jackie helped lead the Dodgers to a National League pennant. Jackie Robinson set records for stolen bases and won the National League's Most Valuable Player Award in 1949. But his greatest success was in paving the way for many other young African American baseball players to play in the major leagues. He retired from baseball in 1957.

Guided Questions

What topics do both passages have in common?

_____

_____

_____

What do these passages tell you about prejudice against African Americans in baseball?

_____

_____

_____

_____

_____

_____

Answer and discuss these questions about the passages. Writing tips based on the questions are given in parentheses.

1. How are these two passages alike and how are they different?

    _____

    _____

    _____

    _____

    (Writing Tip: Whether you are thinking about a topic for a paper or researching a specific topic, take time to gather a little information for your own background knowledge and understanding, even if you don't end up using it in your paper.)

2. Integrating the information in both passages, why do you think the East-West game was more popular than the World Series?

    _____

    _____

    _____

    (Writing Tip: The information you gain by reading texts with different points of view will help you write a more interesting and informative paper.)

3. How could both sources be used in a paper, and why might you want to do so?

    _____

    _____

    _____

    _____

    (Writing Tip: Using a variety of texts can offer different perspectives. The more sources you use, the more interesting facts and recollections on the subject you will have.)

On Your Own

As you read these two passages about the western screech owl, think about how they each approach the topic.

Source 1: Western Screech Owls

The western screech owl is a small owl, about 7 to 10 inches tall. Screech owls have ear tufts and large yellow eyes. They are nocturnal, which means they hunt at night between sunset and dawn, using their excellent eyes and hearing to catch their prey. As carnivores, they eat mice, rats, and squirrels, and also quail and large insects.

When they spot their prey, they will quickly dive down, grab it with their talons, and swoop back up to a tree. They eat small prey in one gulp but will use their talons to eat larger animals. They nest in the cavities of trees but also use nesting boxes and farm sheds. They make good neighbors by doing their part to control the mice population.

Source 2: Western Screech Owls

If you live in a wooded area where western screech owls nest, you can build a nesting box like my dad and I did. Screech owls don't construct a nest. Instead, they often build nests in the cavities of trees. They also use nesting boxes or take over the nests of other cavity-nesting birds such as woodpeckers. They use leaves, feathers, and rotted wood chips to make a soft bed for the eggs. The 16-inch-high nesting box should be plain with no perch. The opening should be around three to four inches in diameter. We placed the box about 10 to 20 feet high on a tree and put a few wood chips in the bottom of the box. Western screech owls usually lay two to seven white eggs. The female sits on the eggs for about 26 days. The eggs may hatch over a period of two to three weeks. During the time the female is on the nest, the male brings her food. Both parents bring food to the young. The young leave the nest about four weeks after hatching, and according to my calculations, that should be any day now!

Complete the following activities.

1 What are some of the differences between the first and second passages?

_____

_____

_____

2 In what kind of text would you probably find each passage, and why?

_____

_____

_____

_____

3 The writing in the second passage feels friendlier because it is written in

A one paragraph.

B third-person point of view.

C direct quotations.

D first-person point of view.

4 The second passage would be useful for readers who want

A step-by-step directions on building a western screech owl birdhouse.

B background knowledge on the nesting habits of all owls.

C examples of different types of birdhouses used in the western states.

D information for a report on owl species and habitats in the Pacific Northwest.

Discuss

5 Discuss with a partner what facts you would recommend adding to the first passage to make it even stronger. Remember to listen carefully to each other's ideas.

_____

_____

_____

_____

 Measuring Up® to the New York Common Core

6 If you were to add a third passage on the western screech owl, what information might it have to make it useful in a different way from either of these two passages?

_____

_____

_____

_____

 7 On a separate piece of paper, write the update on the young western screech owls leaving their nest and flying for the first time. Do a little background research if necessary before you begin to write your description. Then lead a small group discussion about your topic. At specific points, encourage your listeners to pose questions to help clarify what you said.

RI.4.4	Determine the meaning of general academic and domain-specific words or phrases in a text relevant to a grade 4 topic or subject area.
RI.4.10	By the end of year, read and comprehend informational texts, including history/social studies, science, and technical texts, in the grades 4–5 text complexity band proficiently, with scaffolding as needed at the high end of the range.
SL.4.4	Report on a topic or text, tell a story, or recount an experience in an organized manner, using appropriate facts and relevant, descriptive details to support main ideas or themes; speak clearly at an understandable pace.
W.4.3	Write narratives to develop real or imagined experiences or events using effective technique, descriptive details, and clear event sequences. **d.** Use concrete words and phrases and sensory details to convey experiences and events precisely.
CCR.R.4	Interpret words and phrases as they are used in a text, including determining technical, connotative, and figurative meanings, and analyze how specific word choices shape meaning or tone.

Understand the Standards

Literature
Connection

Word choice counts! The English language is full of clever sayings and subtle meanings. Sometimes the word you choose has a **connotative meaning**, an unspoken meaning, emotion, or association. The connotative meaning goes well beyond its dictionary definition, or **literal meaning**.

> **Words to Know**
> connotative meaning
> literal meaning
> figurative meaning
> technical meaning

Is it better to be *slim* or *skinny*? Would you rather be described as *stubborn* or *persistent*? Fill in the chart with a word or words that have a similar literal meaning to each word shown but a positive (or negative) connotative meaning.

Positive Connotation	Negative Connotation
thrifty, frugal	
	stench, stink
stare	
	outdated, obsolete
fatigued, tired	

Connotative meanings don't have to be positive or negative. For example, we have many words that mean roughly the same thing as *vacation*. Each has its own set of associated feelings. How many of these "vacation words" can you name?

Figurative language uses exaggerations or comparisons to get across the meaning in a way that is different from the literal interpretation. Think about the literal meaning of these examples as you explain the **figurative meaning**. In poetry and descriptive nonfiction writing, figurative language helps paint a picture of a place or event. It makes descriptions more interesting and vivid.

Keep your eye on the ball.
I felt like I could run forever.
Mom said my eyes were bigger than my stomach.
He ached for summer vacation to start.

The **technical meaning** of a word refers to a special meaning for the word or phrase in an area such as mathematics, science, or education that may be different from its everyday use. For example, the word *bug* means "error" in the world of computers, "illness" in the medical field, and a type of insect if you're speaking to a biologist.

Guided Instruction

Here is some technical writing on space. Which words or phrases have specific technical meanings in this field? Do any of them have other meanings in regular usage?

The Vocabulary of Space

Science Connection

Our fascination with space started thousands of years ago. Ancient people looked up into the sky and made up stories about the dazzling lights they saw there. They observed the tails of comets and shooting stars that seemed to fall from the sky. During the Renaissance, people began to calculate the orbit of planets around the sun. The invention of the telescope enabled scientists to see into the sky.

Between 1959 and 1971, we traveled outside the bounds of Earth's gravity. Manned spacecraft were sent to explore the moon, and spacecraft have since landed on Venus, Mercury, and Mars. Scientists have observed planets, comets, and asteroids. Special missions and instruments have successfully collected data and samples for further study.

The search goes on. In August 2011, the *Juno* spacecraft lifted off on its way to Jupiter. The spacecraft will arrive in July 2016. During that year it will orbit the planet 32 times. The data collected will answer questions about how Jupiter formed, how much water is in its atmosphere, and how Jupiter's magnetic force field affects its atmosphere.

Guided Questions

What is the general topic of this passage? How does knowing the topic help you decide which meanings of words to use?

_____

_____

_____

_____

_____

Does the writer use words with strong figurative and connotative meanings or words with more literal meanings? Why?

_____

_____

_____

_____

_____

Answer and discuss these questions about the passage.

1. How does what you already know about a tail enable you to visualize the tail of a comet?

_____

_____

_____

_____

2. What is the general meaning of the word *atmosphere*? How is the technical meaning of the word different?

_____

_____

_____

_____

Sports Connection

3. What technical vocabulary is used in various sports? List some words that have special technical meanings and the sport that's associated with each word.

_____

_____

_____

_____

On Your Own

Whether you are writing or speaking, the words you use count. You probably know from experience that you can hurt someone's feelings by accident, just by the wrong choice of words. In writing you often want to get across a specific idea or impression. The passage below describes a hike in the desert. As you read, think about how the author's words help communicate the feeling and experience of this landscape.

Science
Connection

A Hike in the Mojave Desert

My lips, eyes, and ears were painted with gritty sand, making me a crusty, cracked, and aged shadow of my former self. My skin felt like it had metamorphosed into that of the desert horned lizard that curiously poked his head out of his burrow to observe me.

Everything moves in slow motion in the Mojave Desert. Maybe it's because of the searing heat that smacks you into submission, imprinting tiny dots on every inch of your skin with a sizzling sound. Or maybe it's because your brain slows to a snail's pace in such a mesmerizing, brown landscape. There is no canopy, no place to rest or to escape the sun's rays that burn holes through your clothing. Even with a hat on, the water my dad poured over my parched scalp felt like a trickle when I wanted a downpour.

Nothing smart stands out (or up) here. Plants hug the ground for dear life. Trees are small and thick as if to brace themselves. Most animals are nocturnal. They spend their days waiting for the cool of the evening to venture out. A few raptors made lazy circles above us. Did I, Marcus, look like prey? I hoped not, but still, I began to walk a little faster toward our campground.

Complete the following activities.

1 What does the author compare his skin to in this passage, and how does it help get across the author's message?

_____

_____

_____

2 How do you think that you, as a writer, could begin to write in a descriptive way like this about nature?

_____

_____

_____

_____

_____

_____

3 The writing in this passage is effective because it uses a lot of

A technical terms.

B figurative language.

C literal words.

D background knowledge.

4 The words _burrow_ and _canopy_ are

A idioms.

B technical words.

C synonyms.

D figurative words.

Discuss

5 Rewrite the first paragraph of "A Hike in the Mojave Desert" using only literal language, and then discuss with your partner why it is more or less effective than the original.

_____

_____

_____

_____

6 What form of descriptive writing is used in tall tales such as "Paul Bunyan," and why do you think it's used so much?

_____

_____

_____

_____

7 With a partner, discuss your favorite environments or places in nature. Choose one and write a paragraph describing it. Underline any technical words you include and highlight the descriptive language used to help convey the feeling of the place. When you both finish, read your paragraph aloud to your partner. Speak clearly and at an appropriate pace. Then discuss which descriptive parts you liked best in each other's writing and why. Take turns helping each other think of places where more descriptive language might be added. Then rewrite your paragraphs to include the new descriptions.

Peoples Education   Chapter 4 • Reading Informational Texts   **165**

Create a "Weather Report"

The English language contains many weather-related expressions.

- *It's raining cats and dogs!*

- *Ellie is such a fair-weather friend.*

- *He was completely snowed under by all the homework.*

- *Don't rain on my parade!*

Begin by brainstorming with your small group different kinds of weather, such as rain, wind, or snow. Then list examples of figurative language related to those weather words. Invite your parents and friends to add their ideas. When your group has compiled a list of at least 10, create a chart titled WEATHER REPORT. List all the terms on the chart. Choose the best ones to illustrate and display the chart in the classroom.

Write Better Directions

It can be hard to read directions and figure out how to do something new. Now you are in charge of the directions! Discuss as a group how to improve written directions. Will they speak directly to your audience? Will they be fun, or even funny, to read? Will they explain important technical words?

First, choose something you want to explain step by step. It might be how to cook something special, how to play a game, or how to clean up a really messy room! Use the chart below to list any figurative language and technical words that might be useful or fun to include.

Figurative Language	Technical Words and Phrases

Next, work together as a group to write your instructions, using many of the words and phrases on your chart to add interest and perhaps humor. Determine what information is necessary. Test your instructions and revise as necessary. Then read them to the class.

Develop a Convincing Plan

Real World Connection

In a small group, think of something that's very important to people your age. Maybe you'd like a vacant lot fixed up and made into a ball field. Perhaps you wish there was a community swimming pool. Maybe you'd like the bookmobile to stop in your neighborhood each week. Whatever it is, how can you convince the adults who make decisions that the idea is doable?

Begin by agreeing on an idea. Research what facts are available. Has anyone tried to do this before? If so, what stopped it? Who supports the idea? Who doesn't, and why? Whose voices are being heard, and whose opinions aren't? What new information and evidence do you need?

After you've used all your information to make a plan, it's time to present it to the community. Turn the information you've collected, including charts, maps, time lines, photos, and interviews, into a presentation to share with the city council or other community group. Remind everyone that you are all there to listen respectfully to each other's ideas. Win or lose, pat yourselves on the back for being involved members of the community.

Design an Educational Game

Critical Thinking

In a small group, start by discussing what kind of educational game you want to create. What skill do you want to teach and for what grade level? What is the purpose and main idea of your game? Maybe you want to create a game to help second-graders learn a simple science concept or math skill. Research other board games to see how they approached their subject. What creative "theme" will make your game different, visually interesting, and fun to play? How will players move from place to place? What do you have to do to win?

Organize all your information and then create the game, testing it as you go. When you think you're done, test it out one last time and then revise based on comments from team members. When you're done with the final full-color version, invite another group to play or, better yet, head down to the second-grade classroom!

Lesson 33

Argument (Opinion) Writing

W.4.1	Write opinion pieces on topics or texts, supporting a point of view with reasons and information.
	a. Introduce a topic or text clearly, state an opinion, and create an organizational structure in which related ideas are grouped to support the writer's purpose.
	b. Provide reasons that are supported by facts and details.
	c. Link opinion and reasons using words and phrases.
	d. Provide a concluding statement or section related to the opinion presented.
W.4.4	Produce clear and coherent writing in which the development and organization are appropriate to task, purpose, and audience.
W.4.5	With guidance and support from peers and adults, develop and strengthen writing as needed by planning, revising, and editing.
W.4.9	Draw evidence from literary or informational texts to support analysis, reflection, and research.
	a. Apply grade 4 Reading standards to literature.
CCR.W.1	Write arguments to support claims in an analysis of substantive topics or texts, using valid reasoning and relevant and sufficient evidence.
CCR.W.4	Produce clear and coherent writing in which the development, organization, and style are appropriate to task, purpose, and audience.
CCR.W.5	Develop and strengthen writing as needed by planning, revising, editing, rewriting, or trying a new approach.
CCR.W.6	Use technology, including the Internet, to produce and publish writing and to interact and collaborate with others.
CCR.W.7	Conduct short as well as more sustained research projects based on focused questions, demonstrating understanding of the subject under investigation.
CCR.W.8	Gather relevant information from multiple print and digital sources, assess the credibility and accuracy of each source, and integrate the information while avoiding plagiarism.
CCR.W.9	Draw evidence from literary or informational texts to support analysis, reflection, and research.
CCR.W.10	Write routinely over extended time frames and shorter time frames for a range of tasks, purposes, and audiences.

Understand the Standards

Switch on the TV in election season, and you may hear someone say something like this.

Social Studies Connection

> In order to have safe neighborhoods, we need to involve young people. Our youth have too much free time for getting into trouble. We need more jobs for teenagers, more rec centers, and more tutoring programs.

Words to Know
opinion
point of view
reason

This politician is trying to convince you of something. He thinks that giving young people more to do will make neighborhoods safer. This may or may not be true. It is what he believes. He is presenting his opinion.

When you write an opinion, you write from your own point of view. You give reasons to explain why you feel the way you do.

○ An **opinion** is what someone thinks or believes.

    We need to involve young people our neighborhoods.

○ A **point of view** is a way of looking at or thinking about something.

○ A **reason** is a statement that explains something.

    Our youth have too much free time for getting into trouble.

Argument (Opinion) Prompt

Writing Connection

> What is one improvement that you would like to see in your neighborhood? Write an essay to convince your local government to make that change. Start with a strong opinion statement. Give reasons for your opinion. Support your reasons with facts and details. End with a statement that ties your ideas together.

Planning

Purpose and Audience

Before you begin to write, think: Why am I writing? Who will read my work? Always consider your purpose and audience before you begin.

Use the prompt to answer these questions.

1. Why are you writing an opinion essay?

_____

2. Who is your audience?

_____

Prewriting

When you write an opinion essay, you start by stating your opinion. You follow that with reasons that support your opinion.

For this prompt, first brainstorm some ideas for improvements in your neighborhood. Then pick the one you think is most important. Circle it.

My List of Possible Improvements

Once you have chosen a topic, figure out the reasons why that improvement is important. List your reasons.

My Improvement: _____

_____

Reason 1: _____

_____

Reason 2: _____

_____

Reason 3: _____

_____

Drafting

Organizing

Make choices as you write. Begin with a topic sentence. Put your reasons in an order that makes sense to you. You may want to put them in order from most to least important.

Selena drafted a response to the prompt. She decided to use this organization.

> I. Introduction: We need a community garden.
>
> II. Reason 1: Gives the community good, fresh food.
>
> III. Reason 2: Gives kids something to do in the summer.
>
> IV. Reason 3: Brings people together.
>
> V. Conclusion

Selena's plan came right out of her prewriting. She will write one paragraph for each Roman numeral.

Answer these questions about Selena's organization.

1. How many paragraphs will be in Selena's essay? _____

 Measuring Up® to the New York Common Core

2. How many reasons will Selena include in her essay? _____

3. If Selena had just two strong reasons, how many paragraphs would she write?

_____

Linking Words and Phrases

You can use many different words to connect your ideas. This box shows some examples.

for instance	in addition	in order to

Read Selena's introduction. Notice that her introduction touches on her reasons. She will explain each reason in more detail in later paragraphs.

> I would like to see a community garden grow in our
>
> neighborhood. It could provide fresh food and give us
>
> something to do in the summer. In addition, a community
>
> garden is a great way to bring people together.

Answer these questions about Selena's introduction.

1. Which reason did Selena introduce with the words *in addition*?

_____

2. How do the words *in addition* connect the third sentence to the second sentence?

_____

_____

Revising and Editing

Revising for Content and Argument

After you write, read your work. Have a classmate or an adult read it, too. Use this checklist to see what you might fix.

Selena made some changes to the second paragraph of her essay. Read what she changed.

> Our community ~~could use~~ *needs* a garden to give us a
>
> source of fresh food. Right now, the grocery stores in the
>
> neighborhood do not have much produce. *for example, Red's only has old plantains.*

Answer these questions about the edited version of Selena's paragraph.

1. How is *needs* a stronger word than *could use*?

_____

_____

2. What fact did Selena add? How might that help to convince her audience?

_____

_____

Revising for Clarity and Style

When you revise for clarity and style, you make sure your meaning comes through. You make sure you are using words that are right for your reader.

Selena made a few changes to paragraph 3 of her essay. Read her changes.

Children and teens
~~Kids~~ could work in the community garden. This would
∧

give them an activity that is better than hanging out.

Answer these questions about Selena's edited paragraph.

1. Why did Selena change the word *kids*?

_____

2. What might Selena say instead of *hanging out*?

_____

Proofreading

Remember that you are writing for an audience. Be sure to fix any mistakes before you share your work.

Read Selena's conclusion. Notice that her conclusion reminds readers of all her important ideas. Use the appendix on proofreading marks to proofread the paragraph.

PROOFREADING CHECKLIST

❏ Did I indent my paragraphs?

❏ Did I use capital letters correctly?

❏ Did I use punctuation marks correctly?

❏ Did I spell all words correctly?

    A community garden would be a good use of time and

mony. The fresh food healthy activity, and community

spirit it would bring to the neighborhood would help

everone.

Publishing

When you publish your writing, you share it with the public. The public is your audience.

A politician often makes speeches. Selena decided to present her idea as a speech for the city council.

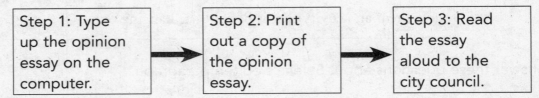

Step 1: Type up the opinion essay on the computer. → Step 2: Print out a copy of the opinion essay. → Step 3: Read the essay aloud to the city council.

Collaborative Learning

Work with a partner. Try reading Selena's speech aloud. Read with emotion. Make your voice sound convincing. Then trade places and listen to the speech. Talk it over. Is it a good, convincing speech? Could it be better? How?

> We Need a Community Garden
> by Selena A.
>
> I would like to see a community garden grow in our neighborhood. It could provide fresh food and give us something to do in the summer. In addition, a community garden is a great way to bring people together.
>
> Our community needs a garden to give us a source of fresh food. Right now, the grocery stores in the neighborhood do not have much produce. For example, Red's only has old plantains and lemons.
>
> Children and teens could work in the community garden. This would give them an activity that is better than wasting time.
>
> The garden could be a place for neighbors to meet, chat, and work together. This would build good community spirit.
>
> A community garden would be a good use of time and money. The fresh food, healthy activity, and community spirit it would bring to the neighborhood would help everyone.

 Measuring Up® to the New York Common Core

On Your Own

 Choose one of these prompts. Write your own opinion essay. Follow the steps in this lesson.

A TV INTERVIEW	A BUSINESS LETTER
1. Imagine that you are going to be interviewed on TV. The question the interviewer will ask is: "From your point of view, what is one thing that should change at your school?" Write a response to the question. Write your opinion and support it with sensible reasons and details. When you are finished, work with two friends. Have one friend "interview" you and the other record your interview.	**2.** Think of a product that has annoyed you in some way. For example, it could be a toy that broke, a pair of uncomfortable shoes, or a food that did not look the way it did on the package. Write a letter to the company that makes the product. Tell your opinion of the product and give clear reasons for your opinion. If you want the company to refund your money or improve the product, tell why.
A REVIEW	**A RESPONSE TO LITERATURE**
3. What is your favorite TV show? Why do you like it? Write a review for your school magazine. Explain what is so great about the show you like. Give specific details and reasons that support your opinion. Try to convince your classmates to watch the show.	**4.** Choose a passage from Chapter 3 of this book. Read it carefully. Then write your opinion of the passage. Consider the plot, characters, setting, and writing style. Use details from the passage to support your opinion.

Informative/Explanatory Writing

W.4.1	Write opinion pieces on topics or texts, supporting a point of view with reasons and information. **d.** Provide a concluding statement or section related to the opinion presented.
W.4.2	Write informative/explanatory texts to examine a topic and convey ideas and information clearly. **a.** Introduce a topic clearly and group related information in paragraphs and sections; include formatting, illustrations, and multimedia when useful to aiding comprehension. **b.** Develop the topic with facts, definitions, concrete details, quotations, or other information and examples related to the topic. **c.** Link ideas within categories of information using words and phrases. **d.** Use precise language and domain-specific vocabulary to inform about or explain the topic. **e.** Provide a concluding statement or section related to the information or explanation presented.
W.4.3	Write narratives to develop real or imagined experiences or events using effective technique, descriptive details, and clear event sequences. **c.** Use a variety of transitional words and phrases to manage the sequence of events.
W.4.4	Produce clear and coherent writing in which the development and organization are appropriate to task, purpose, and audience.
W.4.5	With guidance and support from peers and adults, develop and strengthen writing as needed by planning, revising, and editing.
W.4.6	With some guidance and support from adults, use technology, including the Internet, to produce and publish writing as well as to interact and collaborate with others; demonstrate sufficient command of keyboarding skills to type a minimum of one page in a single sitting.
W.4.7	Conduct short research projects that build knowledge through investigation of different aspects of a topic.
W.4.8	Recall relevant information from experiences or gather relevant information from print and digital sources; take notes and categorize information, and provide a list of sources.
W.4.9	Draw evidence from literary or informational texts to support analysis, reflection, and research. **b.** Apply grade 4 Reading standards to informational texts.
W.4.10	Write routinely over extended time frames and shorter time frames for a range of discipline-specific tasks, purposes, and audiences.
CCR.W.2	Write informative/explanatory texts to examine and convey complex ideas and information clearly and accurately through the effective selection, organization, and analysis of content.
CCR.W.4	Produce clear and coherent writing in which the development, organization, and style are appropriate to task, purpose, and audience.
CCR.W.5	Develop and strengthen writing as needed by planning, revising, editing, rewriting, or trying a new approach.
CCR.W.7	Conduct short as well as more sustained research projects based on focused questions, demonstrating understanding of the subject under investigation.
CCR.W.8	Gather relevant information from multiple print and digital sources, assess the credibility and accuracy of each source, and integrate the information while avoiding plagiarism.
CCR.W.9	Draw evidence from literary or informational texts to support analysis, reflection, and research.
CCR.W.10	Write routinely over extended time frames and shorter time frames for a range of tasks, purposes, and audiences.

Understand the Standards

Before you go off to school, you may listen to a weather report. The reporter gives facts and information about the weather in your area. He or she may use maps and pictures to illustrate the report.

> **Words to Know**
> inform
> explain

Science Connection

Today will be cloudy, with a 60 percent chance of rain.
We expect a high temperature of 60 degrees, starting this morning from a low of 42.

We listen and read for information every day. We ask ourselves questions: "How hot is it?" "Can I eat lunch outside?" "Should I take an umbrella?" Then we look for information that gives us answers. We may find the information we need on TV, on the radio, online, in newspapers, in books, and so on.

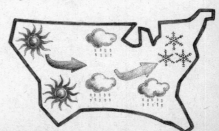

- When you write to **inform**, you give facts about a topic.

- When you write to **explain**, you tell how something is made or done.

Informative/Explanatory Prompt

Writing Connection

> What is the worst form of weather that your area gets? It may be a blizzard, a hurricane, or a tornado. It may just be a bad rainstorm. Imagine that a neighbor is new in town. She wants to know about your area's worst weather. Find out about bad weather in your area. Write a short report that gives the new neighbor information about what to expect.

Planning

Purpose and Audience

Informative/explanatory writing may have one of two purposes: to explain or to give information. Your audience is the person or group that will read your writing.

Use the prompt to answer these questions.

1. Why are you writing a report?

   _____

2. Who will read your report?

   _____

Prewriting

To write an informative report, you must use outside sources. Where could you find information about bad weather in your area? Name two sources.

_____

_____

Colin found a lot of information by talking to neighbors and reading on the Internet. Read Colin's notes. Notice that he uses quotations from real people.

Blizzards in Northfield

1978—over 30 inches, plows could not get through for three days, Mr. Hansen says, "I had to dig a tunnel to my car."

blizzard: snow with wind over 35 mph

1947—drifts 10 feet high, had to dump snow in river, Mrs. Mills remembers, "We had to burn wood because the coal truck could not get through."

1998—warm weather turned blizzard to ice storm, no power for nearly a week

Think about an order Colin could use to write a good report. Number each of his notes in an order that makes sense.

Drafting

Organizing

Once you have notes and have organized them, you are ready to write.

Here is Colin's plan for writing. Each Roman numeral will be a paragraph.

I. What Is a Blizzard?

II. The Blizzard of 1947

III. The Blizzard of 1978

IV. The Blizzard of 1998

V. Conclusion

Look back at Colin's notes. Then answer these questions about his plan.

1. Where will Colin tell about drifts 10 feet high? _____

2. Where will Colin tell about an ice storm? _____

3. Colin's neighbor moved here from Florida. Why might paragraph 1 be important for her?

_____

Linking Words and Phrases

You can use many different words to connect your ideas. This box shows some examples.

also	another	because	for example

This is the introduction to Colin's report. Notice his definition of *blizzard*.

> Because we live in the Northeast, blizzards are the worst kind of weather we get. A blizzard is a snowstorm with winds over 35 miles per hour. There was a big blizzard in 1947 and another 31 years later. There was also a terrible blizzard in 1998.

Answer these questions about Colin's paragraph.

1. What linking word did Colin use to link the blizzards of 1947 and 1978?

_____

2. What linking word did Colin use to connect the first two blizzards to the one in 1998?

_____

Revising and Editing

Revising for Content and Argument

After you write, read your work over to be sure you have said all you mean to say. Have a classmate or an adult read it, too. Use this checklist to see what you might fix.

Read paragraph 2 of Colin's report. Look at the changes he made.

> REVISING INFORMATIVE/
> EXPLANATORY WRITING
> ❏ Is my topic clear?
> ❏ Did I use facts, details, definitions, and quotations to give information?
> ❏ Did I include any information that is not important?

> The blizzard of 1947 led to ~~deep~~ snowdrifts. *over 10 feet deep*
>
> There was so much snow they had to dump it in the
>
> river. Mrs. Mills remembers it well. "We had to burn wood *coal*
>
> because the truck could not get through," she told me.

Answer these questions about Colin's edited paragraph.

1. What word did Colin add to the quotation? Why is that word important?

_____

2. Why did Colin make the change in sentence 1?

_____

Revising for Clarity and Style

Revise your writing to make it clear and easy to read.

Read Colin's conclusion. Look at the changes he made to show how it connects to the rest of the writing.

REVISING INFORMATIVE/ EXPLANATORY WRITING
❏ Did I start with an introduction to the topic?
❏ Are my facts grouped together in paragraphs?
❏ Did I end with a conclusion that sums up the main idea?
❏ Did I use precise language that is right for my audience?

> are the worst weather events that
> As you can see, blizzards happen here.
>   ∧
> dangerous blizzards
> Luckily, ~~storms~~ are rare.
>   ∧

Answer these questions about Colin's edited conclusion.

1. Why did Colin change the first sentence? _____

2. Why did Colin change *storms to blizzards*? _____

Proofreading

Before you finish writing, look for mistakes using this checklist.

PROOFREADING CHECKLIST
❏ Did I indent my paragraphs?
❏ Did I use capital letters correctly?
❏ Did I use punctuation marks correctly?
❏ Did I spell all words correctly?

Use the appendix on proofreading marks to proofread paragraph 3 of Colin's report.

> In 1978, a blizzard left over 30 inches of snow on the streets.
>
> Plows could not get threw for three days. Our neighbor,
>
> mr. Hansen, says, "I had to dig a tunnel to my car.

Publishing

When you publish your writing, you share it with your audience.

A weather reporter publishes his or her work on TV or on the radio. Colin wrote his report for a new neighbor. Here is what he decided to do.

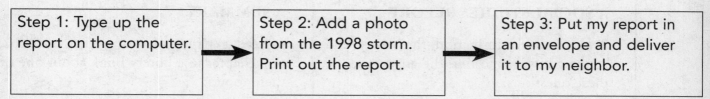

Step 1: Type up the report on the computer.

Step 2: Add a photo from the 1998 storm. Print out the report.

Step 3: Put my report in an envelope and deliver it to my neighbor.

Read Colin's whole report. Look online to find video or photographs of a blizzard in the Northeastern United States. Share your findings with the class.

> ### Blizzards in Northfield
> #### by Colin B.
>
> Because we live in the Northeast, blizzards are the worst kind of weather we get. A blizzard is a snowstorm with winds over 35 miles per hour. There was a big blizzard in 1947 and another 31 years later. There was also a terrible blizzard in 1998.
>
> The blizzard of 1947 led to snowdrifts over 10 feet deep. There was so much snow they had to dump it in the river. Mrs. Mills remembers it well. "We had to burn wood because the coal truck could not get through," she told me.
>
> In 1978, a blizzard left over 30 inches of snow on the streets. Plows could not get through for three days. Our neighbor, Mr. Hansen, says, "I had to dig a tunnel to my car."
>
> The blizzard of 1998 was terrible. It was warm, so the snowstorm turned into an ice storm. Northfield had no power for nearly a week.
>
> As you can see, blizzards are the worst weather events that happen here. Luckily, dangerous blizzards are rare.

On Your Own

 Elevate Choose one of these prompts. Follow the steps in this lesson to do your own informative/explanatory writing.

A WEATHER REPORT

1. Keep track of the weather in your area for a week. Use tools such as thermometers as well as your own senses.

After a week, write a report on what you discovered. Tell your findings in an order that makes sense.

A HOW-TO PARAGRAPH

2. Write a paragraph that tells a young child how to do something you know how to do. It could be anything from making a sandwich to riding a scooter.

Give your paragraph a clear beginning and end, and list all the steps the child should follow in order.

A SOCIAL STUDIES REPORT

3. Use online information, the library, and adults you know to find the answers to these questions:

Who is one famous person who lived in this area long ago? Why is that person famous?

Learn as much as you can about one famous person from your area. Write what you learn in a report that answers the questions.

A SUMMARY

4. Read a chapter of your science textbook, or a chapter in a library book about one of these topics:

- rocks
- plants
- fish

Take notes on the chapter. Think about the main idea.

Use the main idea and several important details to write a one-paragraph summary that tells about what you read. Give your summary a topic sentence. Follow with details that tell about the main idea.

| W.4.1 | Write opinion pieces on topics or texts, supporting a point of view with reasons and information. c. Link opinion and reasons using words and phrases.
d. Provide a concluding statement or section related to the opinion presented. |
|---|---|
| W.4.3 | Write narratives to develop real or imagined experiences or events using effective technique, descriptive details, and clear event sequences.
a. Orient the reader by establishing a situation and introducing a narrator and/or characters; organize an event sequence that unfolds naturally.
b. Use dialogue and description to develop experiences and events or show the responses of characters to situations.
c. Use a variety of transitional words and phrases to manage the sequence of events.
d. Use concrete words and phrases and sensory details to convey experiences and events precisely.
e. Provide a conclusion that follows from the narrated experiences or events. |
W.4.4	Produce clear and coherent writing in which the development and organization are appropriate to task, purpose, and audience.
W.4.5	With guidance and support from peers and adults, develop and strengthen writing as needed by planning, revising, and editing.
W.4.6	With some guidance and support from adults, use technology, including the Internet, to produce and publish writing as well as to interact and collaborate with others; demonstrate sufficient command of keyboarding skills to type a minimum of one page in a single sitting.
W.4.10	Write routinely over extended time frames and shorter time frames for a range of discipline-specific tasks, purposes, and audiences.
W.4.11	Create and present a poem, narrative, play, art work, or literary review in response to a particular author or theme studied in class.
L.4.3	Use knowledge of language and its conventions when writing, speaking, reading, or listening.
a. Choose words and phrases to convey ideas precisely.
CCR.W.3	Write narratives to develop real or imagined experiences or events using effective technique, well-chosen details, and well-structured event sequences.
CCR.W.4	Produce clear and coherent writing in which the development, organization, and style are appropriate to task, purpose, and audience.
CCR.W.5	Develop and strengthen writing as needed by planning, revising, editing, rewriting, or trying a new approach.
CCR.W.6	Use technology, including the Internet, to produce and publish writing and to interact and collaborate with others.
CCR.W.10	Write routinely over extended time frames and shorter time frames for a range of tasks, purposes, and audiences.

Understand the Standards

Some songs tell a story. Singers narrate the story. They use their voices to add emotion to the words they are singing.

Words to Know

entertain

narrative

narrator

personal narrative

sensory details

Black-Jack Davey came a-riding through the woods
And he sang so loud and gaily
Made the woods around him ring
And he charmed the heart of a lady
And he charmed the heart of a lady.

A narrative is a story that may be told in paragraphs, verse, or song. It features characters and the things that happen to them.

- When you write to **entertain**, you try to amuse or interest your reader.

- A **narrative** is a story. It has a beginning, middle, and end.

- A **narrator** is the person who tells a story.

- A **personal narrative** is a true story told by the person who lived it.

- **Sensory details** are words that appeal to the senses.

Narrative Prompt

Writing Connection

> Murphy's Law states, "If anything can go wrong, it will."
> Think of a time when everything seemed to go wrong
> for you. What happened? How did you fix things?
> Who helped you? Write a personal narrative for your
> classmates about that troubled time. Give your narrative
> a clear beginning, middle, and end.

Planning

Purpose and Audience

Before you write, think about your purpose—your reason for writing. Think about your audience—the person or people who will read your work. Understanding your purpose and audience will help you plan how to write.

Use the prompt to answer these questions.

1. Why are you writing a personal narrative?

_____

2. Who will read your personal narrative?

_____

3. Who will be the narrator of your story?

_____

Prewriting

Writing a personal narrative is a lot like writing any story. You need to think about the characters. You need to think about the setting and the plot. You need to tell what happened in an order that makes sense.

Dinh used a story map to write some ideas for his story.

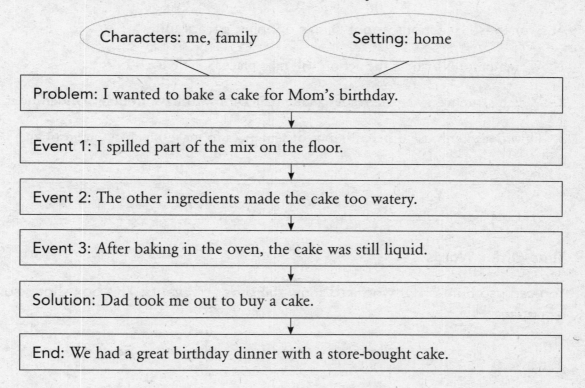

Characters: me, family   Setting: home

Problem: I wanted to bake a cake for Mom's birthday.

Event 1: I spilled part of the mix on the floor.

Event 2: The other ingredients made the cake too watery.

Event 3: After baking in the oven, the cake was still liquid.

Solution: Dad took me out to buy a cake.

End: We had a great birthday dinner with a store-bought cake.

Use Dinh's story map to answer these questions.

1. What is Dinh's story mostly about?

_____

2. How does Dinh's story end?

_____

Drafting

Organizing

Dinh's story map will help him write. His story beginning will introduce the main character, setting, and problem.

> I had the best idea for Mom's birthday. I would bake a cake!
> Never mind that I had never baked before. I had my cake mix and my
> kitchen. <u>What could go wrong?</u>

Answer these questions about Dinh's opening paragraph.

1. Which part tells where the action will take place? Circle it.

2. Which sentence gives the reader a clue that Dinh will have trouble? Underline it.

3. How does Dinh use different kinds of sentences to make his story interesting?

_____

_____

Time-Order Words

You can use time-order words to show the order of events. This box shows some examples.

first	second	then	next
after	before	soon	later

Add time-order words to these sentences in Dinh's story.

_____ I opened the powdery mix. _____ I poured it into a shiny bowl.

Sensory Words

Good writers add sensory words to help readers see, hear, taste, feel, and smell what is happening. Read this part of Dinh's story. Watch for sensory words.

> I opened the powdery mix. I poured it into a shiny bowl.
> Some of it missed and slid onto the tile floor. "Oh, well,"
> I thought.

Answer these questions about Dinh's story.

1. How does the cake mix feel? _____

2. How does the bowl look? _____

3. What kind of floor is in the kitchen? _____

Revising and Editing

Revising for Content and Argument

After you write, read your work. Have a classmate or an adult read it, too. Use this checklist to see what you might fix.

> **REVISING NARRATIVE WRITING**
> ❑ Can my reader tell what is happening in the story?
> ❑ Did I include events that do not fit the main idea?
> ❑ Did I use sensory words to make my story more interesting?

Read the middle of Dinh's story. Look at the changes he made. Notice that he uses his own thoughts as dialogue to show what was going through his mind.

> I added oil and water. The mix looked ~~bad~~ runny. It looked like chocolate soup. "It will harden when it bakes," I thought.

Answer these questions about Dinh's edited paragraph.

1. Why is *runny* a better choice than *bad*?

_____

2. Why did Dinh add the word *chocolate*?

_____

Revising for Clarity and Style

Revise your writing to make it clear and easy to read.

Read the next part of Dinh's story. Notice the changes he made.

> Half an hour later,
> I popped the cake in the oven. I took it out.
>   ∧
>   a disaster
> Now it looked like hot soup. "This cake is ~~bad~~!" I said.
>   ∧

Answer these questions about Dinh's edited paragraph.

1. Why did Dinh add a phrase to sentence 2?

_____

2. What does the change in the last sentence tell you about Dinh's feelings?

_____

Proofreading

Before you finish writing, look for mistakes like the ones listed to the right.

Use proofreading marks in Appendix 2 to proofread the end of Dinh's story.

> Dad took one look at the cake. "Never mind, he said. He
>
> drove me to the store and we picked out an ice-creem cake. That
>
> night, we had a great birthday dinner. With a store-bought cake.

Publishing

Your story is not finished until you share it with your audience.

Songwriters publish their work by having it sung. Dinh decided to share his work in a different way.

Media Connection

Step 1: Type up the story on the computer. → Step 2: Read the story into a recording device. → Step 3: Play back the recording for my classmates.

Work with some friends. Take turns reading aloud a paragraph of Dinh's story. Think about how your voice can show his feelings.

> Mom's Birthday Disaster
> by Dinh V.
>
> I had the best idea for Mom's birthday. I would bake a cake! Never mind that I had never baked before. I had my cake mix and my kitchen. What could go wrong?
>
> First I opened the powdery mix. Next I poured it into a shiny bowl. Some of it missed and slid onto the tile floor. "Oh, well," I thought.
>
> I added oil and water. The mix looked runny. It looked like chocolate soup. "It will harden when it bakes," I thought.
>
> I popped the cake in the oven. Half an hour later, I took it out. Now it looked like hot soup. "This cake is a disaster!" I said.
>
> Dad took one look at the cake. "Never mind," he said. He drove me to the store, and we picked out an ice-cream cake. That night, we had a great birthday dinner with a store-bought cake.

On Your Own

 Choose one of these prompts. Follow the steps in this lesson to do your own narrative writing.

A SONG **1.** Use a tune you like as the basis for your own song-story. Write about a person from history or a character you make up. Tell the story in the verses of the song. When you have the song the way you like it, record it, or have a friend record it. Play it back for your classmates. If you wish, you may also respond to the song-story by writing a short play of creating a video or drawing.	**A FABLE** **2.** A fable is a story that teaches a lesson. Often, fables have animal characters. Write a short fable to entertain a younger child. Decide on the lesson you want to teach. Then work backward to decide how to tell the story. Use animal characters and sensory words.
A SHORT STORY **3.** Use this story starter to write a short story. Use time-order words to tell what happens first, next, and last. Alicia and Brody were hiding in the tree house from the older kids when they heard a strange noise. . . .	**A PERSONAL NARRATIVE** **4.** Has someone told you, "If you can't say something nice, don't say anything at all?" Think of a time when you said something you were sorry for later. What happened? Who was there? How did you feel? How did you fix things? Tell the story in a personal narrative. Give your narrative a clear beginning, middle, and end. Use dialogue and description to make the story interesting.

Writing in Response to Literature

RL.4.11	Recognize, interpret, and make connections in narratives, poetry, and drama to other texts, ideas, cultural perspectives, personal events, and situations.
	a. Self-select text based upon personal preferences.
CCR.W.11	Develop personal, cultural, textual, and thematic connections within and across genres as they respond to texts through written, digital, and oral presentations, employing a variety of media and genres.
W.4.11	Create and present a poem, narrative, play, art work, or personal response to a particular author or theme studied in class.
SL.4.1	Engage effectively in a range of collaborative discussions with diverse partners on grade 4 topics and texts, building on others' ideas and expressing their own clearly.
	e. Seek to understand and communicate with individuals from different cultural backgrounds.

Understand the Standards

When you read actively, you think about the story in front of you and what it means. But you don't just stop there. You decide if you like it. You notice how it makes you feel when you read it. Did it make you think about something similar that has been happening to you? If you feel strongly about it, does it make you want to tell your own story? Does it make you want to draw something or make it into a play you can act out? Responding to literature can take many forms.

Words to Know
response
analyze
point of view
art form

Literature Connection

When you write in **response** to literature, you sometimes write for school and sometimes just for yourself.

When you write for school, you often write to persuade, to inform, to explain, or to entertain.

° You can **analyze** what you read and make connections with other books, poems, or plays.

° You can show how the work helps you understand yourself or other people better, especially people of different backgrounds or **points of view.**

° You can respond creatively. You can create a poem, play, drawing, video, song, or other **art form** the work suggests to your imagination.

Mateo was in the classroom library. He was looking for a book to cheer himself up. He always liked Aesop's Fables. He found one that made him think about himself.

Narrative Prompt

Read the narrative and then the writing prompt.

The Fox and the Stork
by Aesop

A fox once asked a stork to dinner. The stork came. The fox thought it would be fun to play a joke upon the stork. So he gave the stork for his dinner only some thin soup in a flat bowl.

The fox could lap this up like a dog, but the poor stork could not get any soup in his long bill. He went away from the dinner as hungry as he came. The fox laughed to himself to think what a good joke he had played on the stork.

A few days later the story asked the fox to dinner. The fox came, and the dinner was brought in. What do you think the stork had done? He had only soup for dinner. And he had put it into a jar with a long neck. Into this jar the stork put his long bill and ate his fill. The fox could only lick the outside of the jar. He went away as hungry as when he came. He did not laugh at the stork's joke.

> **How does this story make you feel? Are you laughing? Are you upset? Do you agree with the writer's viewpoint? Was the stork being mean to the fox, or was it all just playful and fun? Write a poem, a play, or another personal response to the story that expresses your thoughts or feelings. Then share your response with your classmates.**

Planning

Mateo's buddy Luke liked to play jokes on people. Mateo always laughed, but he never really found them funny. He wanted to write a poem or a story about how people deserve to be treated with respect. He first decided to write a personal response to express how upset practical jokes get him. Then he could decide whether to write this story or write about something else.

Real World Connection

Purpose and Audience

Before you write, think about why you are writing. Think about who will read what you wrote. This will help you prepare to write the best response you can write.

Use the prompt to answer these questions.

1. Why are you writing in response to literature?

_____

2. Who will read your response?

_____

3. What form will your personal response take?

_____

_____

Prewriting

Writing a response to literature is like doing any other kind of writing. You need to plan what you want to say. You think about the work of literature. You tell yourself what you liked and disliked. You tell how something important in the story, poem, or play made you feel. You know you need to express your feelings in an order that makes sense.

Mateo used a chart to organize his ideas.

WHAT I LIKED	WHAT I DISLIKED
how the stork got back at the fox the way the story makes the serving dishes work for animal bodies	It should have said how the stork felt about being tricked and how the fox felt about being tricked back. Aesop's stories usually end with a moral or lesson. This one doesn't. Why? The writer seems to think that getting back at someone is OK.
HOW THE WORK MADE ME FEEL	

HOW THE WORK MADE ME FEEL

I felt annoyed that it didn't say that practical jokes are nasty.

I wanted someone to take my side against practical jokes, and the story didn't. It disappointed me.

Use Mateo's chart to answer these questions.

1. Which responses sound more personal—what he liked or what he disliked?

_____

2. What is Mateo's overall response to the story?

_____

Drafting

Organizing

Mateo's chart will help him write his response. He knows he needs to start with a topic sentence. This sentence will tell readers what his main response to the story is. He can then begin to add details. He remembered that all the details should be related to his topic sentence. He knows that if he gets some good ideas as he writes, he can include them, too.

> "The Fox and the Stork" makes me feel that getting back at someone is OK. I don't think that's right at all. The fox should have thought about the stork's feelings. Instead, the fox just made a fool of him. Is it really OK then for the stork to get back at the fox and make a fool of him, too? I think that's just dumb and mean.

Answer these questions about Mateo's opening paragraph.

1. Which sentence is the topic sentence? Underline it.

2. Does Mateo use facts or opinions to write this paragraph? Why?

_____

_____

3. Mateo is writing for classmates. Why does he say "I think" and "I don't think"?

_____

Adding Details and Evidence

Mateo started to add details in his second paragraph. Notice that they all develop his main idea. They are all on topic.

> My papa always teaches me to show respect for people. That's why I can't do something to get back at Luke when he plays a prank on me. Kids in class make fun of me, but it's not right to be mean to someone. I am not like the stork, who gets even with the fox. Maybe the stork wants to teach the fox a lesson by giving him some of his own medicine. I don't think those two are going to be friends much longer.

Answer these questions about Dinh's story.

1. Why do you think Mateo wrote about showing respect?

_____

2. Why do you think he wonders if the stork wants to teach the fox a lesson?

_____

_____

_____

Revising and Editing

Revising for Content

After you write, read your work. Have a classmate or an adult read it, too. Use this checklist to see what you could fix.

REVISING A RESPONSE TO LITERATURE

❑ Can my reader tell how the work of literature makes me feel?

❑ Do my sentences stay on topic?

❑ Do I refer to the work of literature when I explain my thoughts?

Read Mateo's third paragraph. Notice the changes he made.

I really wish this story said that practical jokes are always

mean and nasty. The fox is mean to the stork. ~~The stork is just as mean back.~~ No one

~~wins. Does the fox ever learn his lesson?~~ He would if I wrote the story, but I don't think the fox does. ~~I wish I could find~~

~~something to cheer me up!~~ Those two could just keep doing

mean things to each other forever until someone gets hurt

from it. It's no fun to have jokes played on you.

Answer these questions about Mateo's edited paragraph.

1. Why does Mateo add the sentence "The stork is always just as mean back"?

_____

_____

2. Why does Mateo cross out the sentence "I wish I could find something to cheer me up"?

_____

Revising for Clarity and Style

Revise your writing to make it clear and easy to read.

> **REVISING A RESPONSE TO LITERATURE**
>
> ❏ Do I have a clear topic sentence?
>
> ❏ Does my ending sound like an ending, or do I just stop?
>
> ❏ Where else are my words unclear?

Mateo reread his planning chart and his response. Then he made some changes to the ending.

This is what I'd tell Fox and Stork. You ~~both~~ don't get it.
The story doesn't show it but
You probably both just got each other angry. Friends should
If you invited me to dinner
treat each other better. That's what I'd do. And P.S. I hate

soup!

How do Mateo's changes improve the last paragraph?

_____

_____

_____

Proofreading

Before you finish writing, look for mistakes like the ones listed to the right.

Mateo made some mistakes when he typed his story on the computer. Use the proofreading marks in Appendix 3 to proofread Mateo's closing paragraph.

PROOFREADING CHECKLIST

❏ Did I indent my paragraphs?

❏ Did I use capital letters correctly?

❏ Did I use punctuation marks correctly?

❏ Did I spell all words correctly?

This is what I'd tell fox and stork. You both don't get it. The

story doesn't show it, but you probly both just got each other

angry. Freinds should treat each other better. That's what I'd do if

you invited me to dinner. And P.S. I hate soup!

Publishing

Your story is not finished until you share it with your audience.

Mateo read the poem "Table Manners" aloud to the class. Then he read his personal response. He asked anyone else who responded to the same poem to read their responses aloud, too.

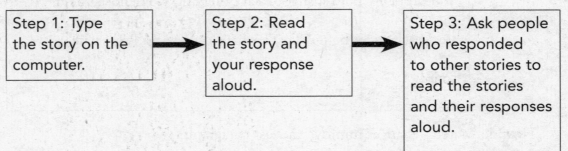

Step 1: Type the story on the computer.

Step 2: Read the story and your response aloud.

Step 3: Ask people who responded to other stories to read the stories and their responses aloud.

Read Mateo's final story.

> Responding to "The Fox and the Stork"
> by Mateo R.
>
> "The Fox and the Stork" makes me feel that getting back at someone is OK. I don't think that's right at all. The fox should have thought about the stork's feelings. Instead, the fox just made a fool of him. Is it really OK then for the stork to get back at the fox and make a fool of him, too? I think that's just dumb and mean.
>
> My papa always teaches me to show respect for people. That's why I can't do something to get back at Luke when he plays a prank on me. Kids in class make fun of me, but it's not right to be mean to someone. I am not like the stork, who gets even with the fox. Maybe the stork wants to teach the fox a lesson by giving him some of his own medicine. I don't think those two are going to be friends much longer.
>
> I really wish this story said that practical jokes are always mean and nasty. The fox is mean to the stork. The stork is just as mean back. No one wins. Does the fox ever learn his lesson? He would if I wrote the story, but I don't think the fox does. Those two could just keep doing mean things to each other forever until someone gets hurt from it. It's no fun to have jokes played on you.
>
> This is what I'd tell Fox and Stork. You both don't get it. The story doesn't show it but you probably both just got each other angry. Friends should treat each other better. That's what I'd do if you invited me to dinner. And P.S. I hate soup!

On Your Own

 Choose one of these prompts. Follow the steps in this lesson to do your own response to literature. Use a chart like the Prewriting chart in this chapter to help you organize your ideas. You may also choose one of the Organizers in the Appendix.

A CREATIVE OR AN ANALYTICAL RESPONSE

1. Write in response to "The Fox and the Stork." Your response can be creative, in the form of a poem or a short play. You could also write an analytical response.

Decide on what the moral of the story is. Then explain how the story develops it. Afterward, draw a picture to go along with your project.

Share your writing and artwork with your classmates.

A RESPONSE TO A TEXT YOU PICK YOURSELF

2. Pick a story, poem, or other work of literature that comes to mind when you read "The Fox and the Stork." Choose a text that tells you something about how people act or behave toward one another. It can be serious or funny.

Summarize what the work is about. Then explain why you agree or disagree with it. Try to persuade readers to side with you.

Share your writing with your classmates.

PUPPET THEATER

3. Create a puppet-theater version of "The Fox and the Stork." Be as simple or elaborate as you wish.

Start by turning the story into a play script. Add a narrator to introduce the story. Write dialogue for your two main characters. Try to get into your characters' heads. Let them turn to the audience and tell their inner thoughts as they serve each other dinner.

Make a video of your play and show it to students in a lower grade.

A "REALLY?" ROUND TABLE

4. Work in a small group to make a list of at least 10 "Really?" statements that state the opposite about how people should act toward each other.

For example, "Sticks and stones can break my bones, but words can never hurt me." "Really?" Then pick the best two or three statements and discuss them. Explain how people from your own cultural background often react. Tell if you agree or disagree.

Listen to one another with openness and respect. Then write a short personal response. Tell the most important thing you learned.

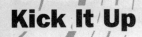

Create a Presentation on Fire Safety

Every town has its own fire department. Firefighters are trained to put out fires and rescue people. What does everyone need to know about fire?

Collaborative Learning

Form a small group with a few classmates. Each person chooses some aspect of firefighting or fire safety and writes an article about it. Here are a few ideas to get you started:

- What kind of training do you need to become a firefighter?

- What should everyone have in their homes in case of fire?

- What is the best way to make sure your pets will be rescued in a fire?

You may want to go to your neighborhood fire station to ask questions. Firefighters are always happy to talk to students about their jobs. Make sure, though, that you arrange a time in advance. An adult can help with this.

Edit your articles to make sure you haven't left out any important information. Use the articles as the basis for a class presentation on fire safety.

Use a Painting to Inspire a Story

Music/Arts Connection

Work with classmates to find these famous paintings online or in a library book. Each student chooses one image to print out or photocopy.

- *Two Little Circus Girls* by Pierre-Auguste Renoir

- *The Sleeping Gypsy* by Henri Rousseau

- *Sudden Shower over Atake Bridge* by Hiroshige

- *The Water Seller of Seville* by Diego Velázquez

Share the images and think about them. What story ideas do they inspire?

Each student chooses one of the images and writes a short story about it. Allow enough time to write, edit, and polish each story before the group meets again to share the stories and talk about them. As you write, ask yourself these questions:

- Have I clearly defined my characters? Do they match the picture?

- Does the action in the picture fit into the plot of my story?

- Have I done a good job of describing the setting in words?

- Does my story naturally arise from what I see in the picture?

Measuring Up® to the New York Common Core

Research National Flags

Multicultural Connection

Work with a small group to create an encyclopedia of national flags.

Each person chooses a different country. Go online or to the library to find an image of the country's flag. Print it out or photocopy it. Research the history of the flag. Here are questions you should answer in your research:

- How long has the country used this flag?

- What colors do you see in the flag? What do the colors mean?

- What does the flag look like? What do the design elements stand for?

- Has the country had other flags before this one? If so, answer the same questions about those earlier flags.

Take a day or two to write, edit, and polish your articles. Once all the articles are finished, use the computer to print out each article. Bind the articles together in a report. Include pictures of the flags as illustrations.

Review a Movie

Discuss

Choose a partner. Watch a movie together in the theater, online, or on DVD. Don't talk about the movie together right away after you see it.

Instead, write a review of the movie. State whether you liked or disliked it. Give the reasons for your reaction. Be as specific as you can. If you saw the movie on DVD or online, you may be able to review parts of it to refresh your memory of the details.

Then, get together with your partner and have a debate about the movie. First, read your review aloud and listen to your partner's. Discuss your reactions to the movie. Do you and your partner agree or disagree? If you disagree, have you both supported your arguments effectively?

Grammar, Usage, and Mechanics Handbook

CCR.L.1/L.4.1: Demonstrate command of the conventions of standard English grammar and usage when writing or speaking.

CCR.L.2/L.4.2: Demonstrate command of the conventions of standard English capitalization, punctuation, and spelling when writing.

Mini-Lesson 1   Relative Pronouns

L.4.1.a   Use relative pronouns and relative adverbs.

- In many complex sentences, a **relative pronoun** introduces a less important idea. Relative pronouns include the words *who*, *whom*, *whose*, *which*, and *that*.

- A relative pronoun refers to a noun earlier in the sentence.

    Examples: Here is a sports article **that** you will like.

- Ms. Sánchez is a teacher **whose** classes are always fun.

- The pots and pans, **which** were old, were thrown out.

- Use *who* as a subject. Use *whom* as the object of a preposition or the object of a verb.

    Examples: Martha, **who** lives in Indiana, calls once a week.

    She is the person to **whom** I wrote that letter.

    Those are the actors **whom** Zach likes best.

 On Your Own

Complete each sentence with the correct relative pronoun. Circle the word or words to which the relative pronoun refers.

1   Is that the boy _____ bike you were riding?

2   Here is the beautiful statue _____ Jesse sculpted.

3 Dr. Albert is the dentist _____ I see.

4 Eva found the sock for _____ she had been searching.

5 Kyle is the student with _____ Olivia is working.

6 The library books _____ we borrowed are due today!

7 The puppies and kittens _____ Bethany saw were cute.

8 My teammates, _____ played well, cried when we lost.

9 Jaime and Gabriela, _____ I had not heard from for a year, came for a visit.

10 The house on the hill, _____ has been empty for a long time, looks spooky.

Mini-Lesson 2   Relative Adverbs

L.4.1.a   Use relative pronouns and relative adverbs.

- In some complex sentences, you can use a **relative adverb** instead of *in which, on which, for which,* or *at which.*

- *Where* often can replace *at which* or *in which.*

   Example: That is the clubhouse **where** we spent our summer.

- *When* often can replace *on which* or *in which.*

   Example: The day **when** the state fair opens is exciting.

- *Why* often can replace *for which.*

   Example: Tell me the reason **why** your report is late.

On Your Own

Complete each sentence. Write the relative adverb that replaces the words in parentheses ( ). Then circle the word to which the relative adverb refers.

1 These are the reasons _____ I cannot come to your party.
(for which)

2 This is the room _____ the school choir practices.
(in which)

3 The day _____ Adam started school was rainy and cool.
(on which)

4 We know the reason _____ Claire won the contest.
(for which)

5 Let's walk to the park _____ the band will perform.
(at which)

6 Did C. J. visit the city _____ her parents met?
(in which)

7 Summer is the season of the year _____ our garden grows.
(in which)

8 During the time _____ we were in Arizona, we saw a place _____
(in which)   (at which)
many movies were filmed.

Mini-Lesson 3   Progressive Verb Tenses

L.4.1.b   Form and use the progressive verb tenses.

- **Tense** is the time that a verb shows. Verbs in **progressive tenses** name ongoing actions. They are made from a form of *be* + a verb with *-ing* at the end.

- The **past progressive tense** shows what was happening some time ago.

  Example: When the fire truck arrived, the flames **were spreading.**

- The **present progressive tense** shows what is happening now.

Example: Joseph **is studying** for tomorrow's math test.

○ The **future progressive tense** shows what will be happening.

Example: I cannot go with you next weekend because my family **will be visiting** my cousins.

 ## On Your Own

Read each sentence. Write the correct progressive tense of the verb in parentheses ( ).

1 Right now we _____ about volcanoes.
(learn)

2 This coming weekend, the Smiths _____ in their garden.
(work)

3 Eric _____ a story when I called.
(read)

4 I see that Jacob _____ his guitar with him again.
(carry)

5 We _____ until we heard the sad news.
(laugh)

6 My cousin Caitlyn _____ college next year.
(attend)

7 While Mom and Dad _____, everyone listened.
(sing)

8 At the moment, I _____ this list of spelling words.
(review)

Mini-Lesson 4   Modal Auxiliaries

L.4.1.c   Use modal auxiliaries to convey various conditions.

○ Some verbs need more than one word to make their meaning clear. They may need a main verb and one or more helping verbs.

○ **Modal auxiliaries** are helping verbs with special meanings. They include *can*, *may*, and *must*.

○ Use *can* when you are talking about an ability.

   Example: Pablo **can** play the trumpet very well.

○ Use *may* when you are talking about a possibility or uncertainty.

   Example: After the movie, we **may** stop for a snack.

○ Use *must* when you are talking about a requirement.

   Example: I **must** finish my homework before I watch TV.

 On Your Own

Read each sentence. Circle the verb choice that makes more sense.

1   Margie (can, may) paint beautiful pictures.

2   The team is winning many games and (must, may) play in the championship game.

3   Becky (can, must) pass a test if she wants to drive a car.

4   If Kevin (can, may) go, we will pick him up at 5:00.

5   Scott and Pam (can, may) run faster than anyone else I know.

6   If she wants to watch TV, Chandra (can, must) make her bed.

7   I don't know if Marcus will come on Saturday. He (may, must) decide to study all weekend.

8   Mom, (can, may) Elena and Luke stay and have supper with us?

Mini-Lesson 5 — Ordering Adjectives

L.4.1.d   Order adjectives within sentences according to conventional patterns.

○ Sometimes you may want to describe a noun with more than one adjective. When you do, put the adjectives in an order that makes sense.

Examples: Last night Al watched a **new funny** TV show. (INCORRECT)

Last night Al watched a **funny new** TV show. (CORRECT)

Mrs. Hamada is buying an **Italian silver used** car. (INCORRECT)

Mrs. Hamada is buying a **used silver Italian** car. (CORRECT)

 On Your Own

Complete each sentence with the adjectives in parentheses ( ). Write the adjectives in the order that makes more sense.

1 A _____ _____ kitten mewed sadly. (gray, tiny)

2 Many people took pictures of the _____ _____ barn. (old, red)

3 Those _____ _____ plants are growing well. (young, three)

4 The _____ _____ pot could not be fixed. (copper, broken)

5 The _____ _____ girl started to cry. (nervous, little)

6 Tyler enjoyed a slice of _____ _____ bread. (fresh, wheat)

7 We saw the _____ _____ vase in a store window. (Chinese, 200-year-old)

8 Jamal, have you and Hannah folded my _____ _____ tablecloth? (cotton, blue)

Mini-Lesson 6   Prepositional Phrases

L.4.1.e   Form and use prepositional phrases.

- A **preposition** is a word that shows the relationship between a noun or pronoun and another word in a sentence.

Examples:

about	for	over
above	from	through
around	in	to
at	near	toward
beside	of	under
by	on	with

- A **prepositional phrase** is made up of a preposition, the object of the preposition (a noun or pronoun), and the words in between the two.

Example: The package **with** the red bow came **from** me.

 On Your Own

Read each sentence. Add a preposition that makes sense. Then underline the entire prepositional phrase. (Each of the last three sentences has two prepositional phrases.)

1 The house _____ the corner is very old.

2 Did you send a party invitation _____ him?

3 We saw a meadow _____ soft green grass.

4 Simon hit the ball and ran _____ first base.

5 Dr. Hall was standing _____ her office, smiling.

6 Those books _____ ancient Egypt are _____ us.

7 Are you stopping _____ the library _____ your brother?

8 The lioness walked _____ her two cubs _____ the blue African sky.

Mini-Lesson 7   Sentence Fragments

L.4.1.f   Produce complete sentences, recognizing and correcting inappropriate fragments and run-ons.

- A **sentence fragment** is an incomplete sentence. It may look like a sentence, but it does not express a complete thought.

- To correct a sentence fragment, decide what part is missing. Then add that part.

    Examples: Were watching TV. (INCORRECT–MISSING SUBJECT)

    My friends and I were watching TV. (CORRECT–ADDED SUBJECT)

    That new cartoon show. (INCORRECT–MISSING PREDICATE)

    That new cartoon show **was very funny.** (CORRECT–ADDED PREDICATE)

    Later that afternoon. (INCORRECT–MISSING SUBJECT AND PREDICATE)

    Later that afternoon, **we had a snack.** (CORRECT–ADDED SUBJECT AND PREDICATE)

 On Your Own

Study each group of words. If it is a sentence, write COMPLETE. If it is a sentence fragment, add the missing part and write the new sentence.

1 Everybody in Nolan's class.

_____

_____

2 Attended the concert last Thursday.

_____

_____

3 Joshua, Kira, and their mother.

_____

_____

4 Kristin won the spelling bee.

_____

_____

5 Must study for the test after supper.

_____

_____

6 We are visiting the museum right now.

_____

_____

7 Made a model of Mars for the Science Fair.

_____

_____

8 On our way to the supermarket last night.

_____

_____

Mini-Lesson 8   Run-on Sentences

L.4.1.f   Produce complete sentences, recognizing and correcting inappropriate fragments and run-ons.

- A **run-on sentence** is two or more sentences that are written together without a comma and conjunction.

- To correct a run-on sentence, write the sentences separately or add a comma and a conjunction (such as *and*, *but*, or *or*).

Example: We wrote a poem about our town the newspaper published it.
(INCORRECT)

We wrote a poem about our town. The newspaper published it.
(CORRECT)

We wrote a poem about our town, **and** the newspaper published it.
(CORRECT)

 ## On Your Own

Rewrite each run-on sentence so that it will be correct.

1 It rained for a while at the fair we had fun anyway.

_____

_____

2 James has the ball he is ready to shoot.

_____

_____

3 Dwayne got a guitar for his birthday now he is taking lessons.

_____

_____

4 Jordan read a book about dolphins she learned a lot from it.

_____

_____

5 I may buy this CD today I may wait for the sale next month.

_____

_____

6 The ripe peaches were juicy and sweet David ate three of them!

_____

_____

7 The science homework was not hard it still took an hour to finish.

_____

_____

8 Laurie planned to stay home instead we talked her into going to the beach with us.

_____

_____

Mini-Lesson 9   Frequently Confused Words

L.4.1.g   Correctly use frequently confused words.

○ Some words sound so much alike that it is easy to confuse them.

Examples: to, too, two   whose, who's
your, you're   where, wear
their, they're, there   here, hear
its, it's   one, won

○ When you write, use these words with care. Be sure that the word you choose has the meaning you want.

Examples: I wanted to play, but Malik was **to** tired. (INCORRECT)

I wanted to play, but Malik was **too** tired. (CORRECT)

That store treats **it's** customers well. (INCORRECT)

That store treats **its** customers well. (CORRECT)

On Your Own

Read each sentence. Circle the correct word from each choice in parentheses ( ).

1 Terry and Lukas will give (their, they're) report tomorrow.

2 I just saw the new movie, and (its, it's) amazing!

3 Alyssa wants (too, to) paint her bedroom purple and green.

4 This form tells you to print all (your, you're) information.

5 Jade worked on homework for (too, two) hours last night.

6 "(Whose, Who's) backpack is this?" Charlie asked.

7 That jacket is the (one, won) that I want to (where, wear) to the party.

8 (Their, There) is the book that (you're, your) always telling us about.

Mini-Lesson 10   Capitalization Rules I

L.4.2.a   Use correct capitalization.

- ○ Capitalize the first word in a sentence.

- ○ Capitalize days of the week, months of the year, and holidays.

- ○ Do not capitalize special occasions that are not holidays.

> **Examples:** **I** think that **V**alentine's **D**ay will fall on **T**uesday, **F**ebruary 14.
>
> **T**his restaurant is closed on **M**ondays, so we will celebrate my **b**irthday at home.

On Your Own

Read each sentence. Circle each word that should begin with a capital letter.

1 heather will spend thanksgiving with her grandparents.

2 i love to watch the leaves change color in october.

3   emily will celebrate her parents' anniversary on june 23.

4   each friday night in april, stores will stay open late.

5   stephen's graduation was on saturday, may 16.

6   a parade marches through town every fourth of july.

7   we honor the military on thursday, november 11—veterans day.

8   are you planning to stay up on new year's eve to see december turn into january?

Mini-Lesson 11   Capitalization Rules II

L.4.2.a   Use correct capitalization.

○ Capitalize the names and titles of people and pets.

○ Capitalize the names of certain places, such as cities, states, and countries.

○ Capitalize the names of certain things, such as buildings, monuments, schools, and organizations.

Examples: Uncle Walt teaches at Lincoln Elementary School in Minneapolis, Minnesota.

His dogs, Comet and Pepper, were a gift from Mr. and Mrs. Morgan, friends of his from Illinois.

He got those dogs after he visited the Field Museum in Chicago with the Morgans.

On Your Own

Read each sentence. Circle each word that should begin with a capital letter.

1   I think that mrs. okada, our neighbor, was born in japan.

2   The griffith observatory is in los angeles, california.

3   We got our cat, snowball, from the polk county humane society.

4   Did megan and joe visit the statue of liberty?

5   Last summer, jesse and grandma claire spent a week in philadelphia.

6   We love dr. reyes, who works for the international red cross in nigeria.

7   My teacher cried, "No, peter! You may not bring izzy, your iguana, to smith elementary school!"

8   The city of cleveland, ohio, is the home of the rock and roll hall of fame.

Mini-Lesson 12   Capitalization Rules III

L.4.2.a   Use correct capitalization.

- Capitalize the first word and the last word in a title.

- Capitalize every noun, pronoun, verb, adjective, and adverb in a title.

- Capitalize a preposition only if it is five or more letters long.

- Do not capitalize any of these words unless they are first in a title: *a, an, the, and, but, or, so.*

  Examples: *A Tour Through the Everglades* (book)

  Lisa Lee and Her Amazing Machines (movie)

  "Look to the Land Where the Sun Never Sets" (poem)

  "My Heart Was Sad, but You Made It Glad" (song)

 On Your Own

Read each title. Circle each word that should begin with a capital letter.

1   *a short history of the supreme court*

2   "will i find you quickly in my dreams?"

3   *the other place, or julie's weird adventure*

4   "a silly poem for a summer afternoon"

5   *traveling to mars—and beyond our solar system*

Mini-Lesson 13   Commas and Quotation Marks

L.4.2.b   Use commas and quotation marks to mark direct speech and quotations from a text.

- Use **quotation marks** to show the words that someone says in direct speech. These words are called a **quotation.**

- Use quotation marks to show the words that are quoted from a text. These words also are called a quotation.

- If the quotation begins a sentence, write a comma before you write the last quotation marks. Then name the speaker.

    Example: "We had a great time at the circus**," Rob said.**

- If the quotation ends a sentence, write a comma after you name the speaker. Then write the last quotation marks after the period.

    Example: The story began, "Once upon a time, a princess lived in a golden castle."

 On Your Own

Write each sentence. Add quotation marks and commas where needed.

1   Mrs. Edwards said Today we will learn about the water cycle.

_____

_____

2   I must leave, or I'll be late for practice Myla explained.

_____

_____

3   We wait for the future to show us the article concluded.

_____

_____

4 Jeremy smiled as he read On the planet Narlatta, everyone could fly.

_____

_____

5 Today is Mom's birthday Dana said. Then she added We are making her a special dinner.

_____

_____

Mini-Lesson 14   Commas in Compound Sentences

L.4.2.c   Use a comma before a coordinating conjunction in a compound sentence.

○ A **compound sentence** expresses two or more complete and equal thoughts.

○ Many times, you can connect the thoughts with a conjunction such as *and*, *but*, *or*, or *so*. When you do, you usually will want to write a comma before the conjunction.

> **Examples:** Anita wants money for a new bicycle, so she will baby-sit for her neighbors.
>
> Did you go to the movies with Ryan, or did you work on your report at home?

 On Your Own

Add commas to these compound sentences where needed.

1 We saw the new display at the museum and it was terrific.

2 Diego was running late so he called his parents.

3 The storm was powerful but it did not damage my house.

4 Katy may be at home or she may have gone to the supermarket.

5 The Ravens won the big game so now they are having a pizza party.

6 Will Mom and Dad come along on our class trip or will Aunt Sofia take Dad's place?

7 Kim went to Amber and Becca's house but both sisters had gone out.

8 Michael stopped at the library and then he went home.

Mini-Lesson 15   Spelling

L.4.2.d   Spell grade-appropriate words correctly, consulting references as needed.

○ Knowing how to spell correctly is important. Here are 75 words that fourth-graders should be able to spell.

addition	flower	praise
amount	follow	prepared
answer	freight	quality
appearance	frown	remember
argument	genius	repair
avenue	glory	roast
basically	growl	scarce
beetle	happiness	season
boast	hundred	serious
bridge	island	sideways
cartoon	journal	squeaky
century	kitchen	strange
continue	kneel	suddenly
creation	knowledge	themselves
crowded	least	throat
cruel	lettuce	tomorrow
dangerous	loyal	trouble
daughter	manage	truthful
definitely	measles	understood
difference	newspaper	unload
earthquake	often	unusual
exciting	people	value
exercise	pillow	vegetable
familiar	position	width
fifth	potatoes	yield

     Measuring Up® to the New York Common Core

On Your Own

Look at the underlined words in each sentence. Circle the word that is spelled incorrectly. Then write the correct spelling on the line. When you need to do so, use a dictionary.

1 My grandmother <u>definately</u> does not like <u>crowded</u> rooms. _____

2 Jennifer is her parents' <u>fifth</u> <u>daugter</u>. _____

3 The workers <u>prepared</u> to <u>unlode</u> the <u>freight</u>. _____

4 Some <u>poeple</u> live for a <u>century</u>—that is, one <u>hundred</u> years. _____

5 A person who does not give a <u>truthful</u> <u>anser</u> may cause <u>trouble</u>. _____

6 <u>Basicaly</u>, crossing that <u>bridge</u> was just too <u>dangerous</u>. _____

7 The <u>potatoes</u> and <u>lettuce</u> at Ed's <u>vegtable</u> stand are of the highest <u>quality</u>. _____

8 Don't those clouds look <u>unusual</u>? What a <u>strange</u> <u>appearence</u> they have! _____

9 <u>Tommorow</u> the <u>newspaper</u> will report the <u>earthquake</u> that hit the <u>island</u>. _____

10 Dr. Patel is very <u>serious</u> about gaining <u>knowlege</u>. He is a <u>genius</u>, and he wants to make a <u>difference</u> in the world! _____

Speaking and Listening Handbook

SL.4.1 Engage effectively in a range of collaborative discussions with diverse partners on grade 4 topics and texts, building on others' ideas and expressing their own clearly.

SL.4.2 Paraphrase portions of a text read aloud or information presented in diverse media and formats, including visually, quantitatively, and orally.

SL.4.3 Identify the reasons and evidence a speaker provides to support particular points.

SL.4.4 Report on a topic or text, tell a story, or recount an experience in an organized manner, using appropriate facts and relevant, descriptive details to support main ideas or themes; speak clearly at an understandable pace.

SL.4.5 Add audio recordings and visual displays to presentations when appropriate to enhance the development of main ideas or themes.

SL.4.6 Differentiate between contexts that call for formal English and situations where informal discourse is appropriate; use formal English when appropriate to task and situation.

CCR.SL.1 Prepare for and participate effectively in a range of conversations and collaborations with diverse partners, building on others' ideas and expressing their own clearly and persuasively.

CCR.SL.2 Integrate and evaluate information presented in diverse media and formats, including visually, quantitatively, and orally.

CCR.SL.3 Evaluate a speaker's point of view, reasoning, and use of evidence and rhetoric.

CCR.SL.4 Present information, findings, and supporting evidence such that listeners can follow the line of reasoning and the organization, development, and style are appropriate to task, purpose, and audience.

CCR.SL.5 Make strategic use of digital media and visual displays of data to express information and enhance understanding of presentations.

CCR.SL.6 Adapt speech to a variety of contexts and communicative tasks, demonstrating command of formal English when indicated or appropriate.

L.4.3 Use knowledge of language and its conventions when writing, speaking, reading, or listening.

Mini-Lesson 1   Speaking in a Group Setting

SL.4.1.a Follow agreed-upon rules for discussions and carry out assigned roles.

SL.4.1.b Come to discussions prepared, having read or studied required material; explicitly draw on that preparation and other information known about the topic to explore ideas under discussion.

CCR.SL.6 Adapt speech to a variety of contexts and communicative tasks, demonstrating command of formal English when indicated or appropriate.

 ### Introduction

Whether you just raise your hand to answer a question or take part in a formal discussion, you want to do your best. You learn from the group and members of the group learn from you. Practice makes perfect. If you try to do your best each time you speak in a class discussion, by the end of the year, you will be an expert at it!

Make It Work

Here are some useful rules to follow. They will make speaking in a group setting easy for you.

- ☐ Always come prepared.
- ☐ Look at your audience.
- ☐ Speak loudly enough so that others can understand you.
- ☐ Speak slowly enough so you don't sound rushed.
- ☐ Speak in full sentences.
- ☐ Use formal English when the setting is formal
- ☐ Speak with expression.
- ☐ Stay on topic.
- ☐ Explain your ideas and answer questions.
- ☐ Do not interrupt other speakers.

 Put It Together

Find a book of short verse and choose one poem to read aloud. Begin by telling why you chose the poem. End by answering one question about it from a classmate. Practice the skills listed in Make It Work.

Mini-Lesson 2 Participating in Discussions

SL.4.1.b	Follow agreed-upon rules for discussions and carry out assigned roles.
SL.4.1.c	Pose and respond to specific questions to clarify or follow up on information, and make comments that contribute to the discussion and link to the remarks of others.
CCR.SL.1	Prepare for and participate effectively in a range of conversations and collaborations with diverse partners, building on others' ideas and expressing their own clearly and persuasively.
CCR.SL.2	Integrate and evaluate information presented in diverse media and formats, including visually, quantitatively, and orally.
CCR.SL.6	Adapt speech to a variety of contexts and communicative tasks, demonstrating command of formal English when indicated or appropriate.

Introduction

Small-group discussions and large-group discussions are an important part of learning. These discussions give you an opportunity to put effective listening and speaking skills into practice.

It's a good idea every year to "discuss how to discuss." If you agree on rules for discussions, you will help them run smoothly for the rest of the year.

Make It Work

Here are some rules that make discussions run smoothly. How would you change them to fit the needs of your class? What other rules would you add? Decide the answers to these questions in a small group. Then as a large group, reach an agreement about which rules work best for your class. Be sure that all ideas and suggestions stay on topic and build on what other students have said.

Here are some rules to start off with:

- ☐ Listen when others are speaking.
- ☐ Wait your turn to speak.
- ☐ Raise your hand to show you want the floor.
- ☐ Speak and listen with respect. Do not make faces or add side comments.
- ☐ Keep to the point.
- ☐ Use appropriate language.
- ☐ Encourage everyone to participate.

You may also want to introduce certain roles in your more formal class discussions. One student can be selected as today's discussion leader. Another student can take notes and report about the discussion to the whole class.

Put It Together

Practice the rules that you agree on. Hold a formal discussion about some event in the news or a topic of interest that you all vote on. Invite a classmate to be a formal observer at your discussion. The observer's job is to point out when speakers and listeners have strayed from the agreed-on rules. Be committed to improving your discussion skills.

Mini-Lesson 3   Listening for Details and Evidence

SL.4.3   Identify the reasons and evidence a speaker provides to support particular points.

SL.4.1.d   Review the key ideas expressed and explain their own ideas and understanding in light of the discussion.

CCR.SL.3   Evaluate a speaker's point of view, reasoning, and use of evidence and rhetoric.

 ## Introduction

Little children learn with all their senses, and if you think about it, so do you. You do a hands-on experiment in science. You listen to a story or speech being read aloud. You view a short video on the computer. You see how something is made, how it works, or what the speaker wants you to think is true. You have many opportunities to listen for details and evidence. Here's how to make the most of these experiences.

 ## Make It Work

You need to be an active listener in order to keep track of the information you hear and decide how important it is. One useful trick is to listen for the speaker's main idea and write it down. Then listen for the details that the speaker gives to explain the main idea. Sometimes in place of details, you may hear the speaker's reasons for thinking it's true. You can use a diagram like this one to keep track of what you hear.

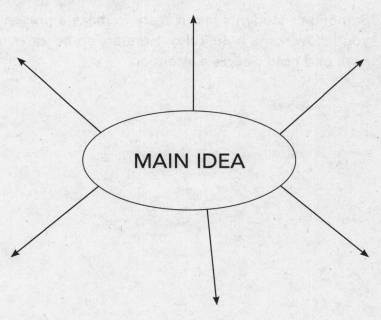

Put It Together

Listen carefully as your teacher reads a passage from one of your schoolbooks or plays a short video for you on the computer. Come prepared to listen actively by having paper to make an organizer like the one in Make It Work. Afterwards, compare your notes with your classmates'. Create a final set of notes about the passage.

Mini-Lesson 4   Making Presentations

SL.4.4	Report on a topic or text, tell a story, or recount an experience in an organized manner, using appropriate facts and relevant, descriptive details to support main ideas or themes; speak clearly at an understandable pace.
SL.4.5	Add audio recordings and visual displays to presentations when appropriate to enhance the development of main ideas or themes.
SL.4.6	Differentiate between contexts that call for formal English and situations where informal discourse is appropriate; use formal English when appropriate to task and situation.
CCR.SL.5	Make strategic use of digital media and visual displays of data to express information and enhance understanding of presentations.
L.4.3.c	Differentiate between contexts that call for formal English (e.g., presenting ideas) and situations where informal discourse is appropriate (e.g., small-group discussion).

 Introduction

Sometimes students find it scary to make a presentation. It's a lot less scary if you follow some basic rules. Here are some ideas for making presentations that grab and hold people's attention.

   Measuring Up® to the New York Common Core

Make It Work

Have something interesting to say. Have an interesting or appealing way to present it.

If you are giving information or telling a story, do this:

☐ Decide how formal the presentation is should be and choose the level of language, formal or formal, that is best for it.

☐ Have an overall plan for the beginning, the middle, and the end.

☐ Stay on purpose when you present information.

☐ Do not stray from the topic.

☐ Give all important facts about the topic.

☐ Add details that help you give the full picture.

☐ Speak clearly and at a pace that will help your listeners understand you.

☐ Use photographs, drawings, audio recordings, and videos to build understanding and hold everyone's interest.

Put It Together

Pick a topic that you feel comfortable with and know something about. It can be related to your hobby, a sport you play, a place you have visited, or something else of interest. Then prepare a five-minute factual presentation about it. Follow the suggestions in Make It Work. Then make your presentation to the class. Remember to include visual aids to hold everyone's interest. Invite classmates' questions and respond to them.

Mini-Lesson 5 Speaking to Inform or Explain

SL.4.2 Paraphrase portions of a text read aloud or information presented in diverse media and formats, including visually, quantitatively, and orally.

CCR.SL.4 Present information, findings, and supporting evidence such that listeners can follow the line of reasoning and the organization, development, and style are appropriate to task, purpose, and audience.

CCR.SL.2 Integrate and evaluate information presented in diverse media and formats, including visually, quantitatively, and orally.

 ## Introduction

Speaking to inform can be done in many different ways. Sometimes you may give someone simple directions. Other times, you may explain in detail how to do or make something. You may share what you learned about a topic and give information you read in books or online. Your purpose in all these instances is to inform.

 ## Make It Work

It always helps to organize your thoughts, even when you are doing something as simple as giving walking directions. Think about what your listener needs to know. How far? When to turn? What landmarks to look for?

When you speak more formally or at greater length, you still need to focus on what your listeners need to know.

☐ Be organized. Make it easy for listeners to follow your thoughts.

☐ Use language that is appropriate for your purpose.

☐ Be clear. Help listeners identify your main ideas.

☐ Be even more clear. Show how reasons and supporting details are connected with your main ideas.

☐ Save words. Paraphrase information from books and other sources instead of reading the whole thing aloud.

☐ Stay on topic.

 ## Put It Together

Work with a partner to make a short presentation about a topic you want to know more about. Do some research first. Collect information, photos, short video clips, and other catchy and informative materials. Define your topic further, and then organize your presentation. Practice it until you feel comfortable with it. Revise it to make it flow smoothly. Then present it to classmates.

 Measuring Up® to the New York Common Core

Mini-Lesson 6   Speaking to Persuade

SL.4.3   Identify the reasons and evidence a speaker provides to support particular points.

CCR.SL.3   Evaluate a speaker's point of view, reasoning, and use of evidence and rhetoric.

CCR.SL.4   Present information, findings, and supporting evidence such that listeners can follow the line of reasoning and the organization, development, and style are appropriate to task, purpose, and audience.

L.4.3.c   Differentiate between contexts that call for formal English (e.g., presenting ideas) and situations where informal discourse is appropriate (e.g., small-group discussion).

 ## Introduction

Your younger brothers and sisters speak to persuade by stamping their feet and shouting "No" as loud as they can. Your listeners are older and expect more from you. They expect reasons and conclusions drawn from evidence. They expect you to convince them and make them want to agree with what you say.

 ## Make It Work

The best way to persuade is to know what your listeners think about a topic. Then show them why they're right to believe that, or convince them that what you suggest is a better choice. Here are three ways to do this:

☐ Give facts and draw conclusions from those facts.

☐ Appeal to your listeners' emotions.

☐ Present yourself as open and fair-minded. Show you respect the other side's point of view. Show why your understanding of the situation is better.

Many arguments contain all three ways to persuade.

 ## Put It Together

Find a topic that you care about. You want to convince listeners that your "take" on the topic is something they should agree with. It can be about a worthy cause you want to support or a situation that upsets you and you want to fix. It can be about policy that could be improved. Gather your arguments and think about the best way to present them. Decide if you should use formal or informal language. Then take part in a classroom discussion. Take turns listening to each other's speeches. At the end of each session, vote on the most convincing speech.

Mini-Lesson 7   Building Awareness of Audience

SL.4.1.e   Seek to understand and communicate with individuals from different perspectives and cultural backgrounds.

Introduction

Not everyone looks like you, dresses like you, or thinks like you. We are all different. We are all individuals. We come from many different cultural backgrounds. Those backgrounds are part of us and make us who we are.

Make It Work

When you are speaking in front of an audience, you need to be aware of the differences among people. Here are some that often stand out. None are "wrong," just "different."

In some cultures...	In other cultures...
• Making eye contact is important. It is a sign of respect.	• Not making direct eye contact is a sign of respect.
• You are expected to get to the point right away when talking.	• You are expected to make informal "small talk" first.
• You stand close to a person.	• You keep some distance between yourself and another person.
• Girls and boys talk as equals.	• Girls and boys are kept apart.
• Being direct is important.	• Being polite is important.

Put It Together

Hold a round table discussion about your favorite holidays and how you celebrate them. Encourage each other to bring in some items for a show and tell. Speak to each other with respect. Do not interrupt. Learn to appreciate what each person speaks about and brings to show.

Organizer 1: Presenting an Opinion

My Choice: _____

Reason 1: _____

_____

_____

Reason 2: _____

_____

_____

Reason 3: _____

_____

_____

Organizer 2: Supporting an Opinion

Opinion:

Reason 1:

Reason 2:

Reason 3:

 Measuring Up® to the New York Common Core

Organizer 3: Sequencing Information

My Notes About _____

Number your notes in an order that makes sense.

Organizer 4: Outline

Title: _____

Paragraph I: Introduction

Paragraph II: _____

_____

_____

Paragraph III: _____

_____

_____

Paragraph IV: _____

_____

Paragraph V: Conclusion

Organizer 5: Creating a Narrative

Characters:

Setting:

Problem:

Event 1:

Event 2:

Event 3:

Solution:

End:

Organizer 6: Telling a Story

PICTURE of the main character and the setting:

What happens FIRST:

What happens NEXT:

What happens LAST:

Proofreading Mark	Meaning	Example
≡	capitalize	we turned left onto ≡ beale street. ≡ ≡
⊙ or ∧̇	add a period	Please call Dr⊙ Jones tomorrow⊙
∧	add something	How much doˆeˢ that ∧ pen cost ? ∧
∧	add a comma	Dinah∧did you call Minnie, Jake∧and Mo?
ˇ˙˙	add quotation marks	She asked, ˇDid you buy any snacks?ˇ
ˇ	add an apostrophe	Donˇt you think Markˇs story is good?
ℓ	take something away	Our class visited Washingtonℓ, DC.

¶	indent the paragraph	¶Once upon a time, a toad lived under a stone wall. Living nearby were a chipmunk and a garter snake.
‾‾‾ ∧	respell or rewrite	Two wrongs do not make a ~~write~~. right
/	make a lowercase letter	Please ask your /Aunt to send me her /Recipe.
move the text	move the text	I looked for my book around the room.

Writing Model 1: Opinion (Argument) Writing

The paragraph begins with a clear topic sentence that states the writer's opinion.

Our school should spend some money fixing up the school entrance. Right now, the entrance looks dirty and dull. That makes people think our school is dirty and dull. It would not take much to make the entrance pretty and lively. For instance, we could plant flowers in large pots, paint the door bright colors, and hang a nice sign with the name of our school. These improvements would do a lot for school spirit.

The writer expresses a point of view ("the entrance looks dirty and dull") and goes on to give a reason for the proposed change ("That makes people think our school is dirty and dull").

The writer uses linking words to introduce examples ("plant flowers," "paint the door," "hang a nice sign").

The paragraph ends with a concluding statement.

Writing Model 2: Informative/Explanatory Writing

Have you ever heard of Patriots' Day? If you live in Massachusetts or Maine, you probably have. It is a holiday there.

> The writer begins by introducing the topic.

Patriots' Day celebrates the first battles in the American Revolution. The Battles of Lexington and Concord happened in 1775. Because the battles took place in April, the holiday is celebrated on the third Monday in April.

> The writer may define terms early in the essay.

People in Boston celebrate Patriots' Day in an unusual way. The Boston Marathon takes place on that day. Runners come from all over the world to run in a 26-mile race.

> Ideas that go together are put into paragraphs. This paragraph is all about the Boston Marathon.

Another way of celebrating takes place in the towns of Lexington and Concord. People there celebrate the day with parades and a make-believe battle.

> Linking words connect ideas that go together (a marathon happens in Boston; parades and battles happen in Lexington and Concord).

On Patriots' Day, offices and schools are closed. Citizens of Massachusetts and Maine take a day to remember their early history.

> A conclusion ties the ideas in the essay together.

Writing Model 3: Narrative Writing

Pablo was the only boy in the neighborhood without a bike. He wanted to ride to the playground with his friends, but he had to run alongside them.

The story beginning introduces the characters, setting, and problem.

"You can use my bike," said his sister Rosa. "It's too small for me."

"Your bike is pink!" said Pablo. "It has flowers pasted onto it! My friends will laugh at me!"

Dialogue between characters helps to move the story along.

Rosa shrugged and walked away. A few minutes later, she came back with a can of shiny black paint and a brush. "It's yours if you want it," she said.

Time-order words and phrases show the order of events.

Sensory details help the reader picture what is happening.

Pablo worked all day. He peeled off the flower stickers and painted that bike. The next morning, he proudly rode to the playground with his friends.

The story ending gives a sense of closure.

These generic scoring rubrics can be used in the evaluation of many types of written responses.

2-Point Rubric

2 Points	A 2-point response is accurate and complete, and fulfills all the requirements of the task. Necessary support and/or examples are included, and the information given is clearly text-based. Any extensions beyond the text are relevant to the task.
1 Point	A 1-point response includes some correct information, but may be too general or overly specific. Some of the support and/or examples may be incomplete or omitted.
0 Points	A 0-point response is inaccurate, confused, and/or irrelevant, or the student failed to respond to the task.

4-Point Rubric

4 Points	A 4-point response demonstrates an understanding of the task, completes all requirements, and provides an insightful or creative response to the prompt. Language and organization are sophisticated. Few or no errors in grammar or mechanics exist.
3 Points	A 3-point response demonstrates an understanding of the task, completes all requirements, and provides an adequate and comprehensive response to the prompt. Language is appropriate, and organization is logical. Few errors in grammar and mechanics exist, and those do not interfere with meaning.
2 Points	A 2-point response demonstrates a partial understanding of the task, completes some of the requirements, and provides an unfinished, inconsistent, or otherwise flawed response to the prompt. Language is simplistic, and organization may be hard to follow. Errors in grammar and mechanics exist.
1 Point	A 1-point response demonstrates minimal understanding of the task, fails to complete all requirements, and only tangentially refers to the prompt. Language is simplistic or inappropriate, and organization is illogical. Multiple errors in grammar and mechanics interfere with meaning.
0 Points	A 0-point response is irrelevant, illegible, incomprehensible, or not in English.

Notes

Notes

English Language Arts — Level D   Copying is permitted.   Measuring Up® to the New York Common Core

Notes

Notes